THE
SOUTHERN WA

C000180719

CONTENTS

© Kevin Robertson (Noodle Books) and the various contributors 2012
ISBN 978-1-906419-89-9
First published in 2012 by Kevin Robertson
under the **NOODLE BOOKS** imprint
PO Box 279
Corhampton
SOUTHAMPTON
SO32 3ZX
www.noodlebooks.co.uk
editorial@thesouthernway.co.uk

Printed in England by
The Berforts Information Press Ltd

Summer time at Woody Bay.

I think we can truly say we have a 'Southern Way' pin-up at last - and what is more it is page 3!

The image was sent by a good friend, Nick Britton, who enquired quite nonchalantly as to its suitability for 'SW'? No hard decisions needed there. It origins are unknown, save for the fact Nick acquired the print from a dealer at a postcard fair - nothing written on the reverse of course. The location was easy, No 759 'Yeo' awaiting departure to Lynton.

I suspect most readers will have a soft spot for the 'L & B' and I can do no more than heartily recommend the new privately published work 'The Lynton & Barstaple Railway Measured and Drawn' by Stephen D Phillips. This contains a view of Woody Bay from the same angle but minus the train (and pin-up).

Copies of the book are available from the L & B website or from our friends at Lightmoor Press. Not cheap but it really is an excellent work.

Stephen Phillips has identified the wagon, "The west side of the elusive No 24 (28303)."

Above - *Having had summer at Woody Bay, why not summer at the opposite end of the Southern system and with it a change in female fashion three decades later. Recorded by J Burke in the days before closure, 15 June 1964, the notes on the reverse state, " Driver Albert Osborne of Tonbridge looks in on a sketching session as he drives one of the last trains on the Bexhill West to Crowhurst branch line, scheduled for closure under the Beeching plan next Monday. The girls, Sonia Belahorska, Jane Barker and Janice Mitchell, all 17-year old Bexhill school girls, sketch the little Sussex station from an already deserted platform."*   *J Burke - with thanks to Mike Thorpe for finding the image.*

Rear cover - *Sporting headcode 30 denoting a Portsmouth Harbour – Brighton via Littlehampton service, this pair of 2 HAPs, with unit No. 6065 leading, runs into Bosham station on the West Coastway line in the late 1970s. They are just about to pass the delightful signalbox and crossing gates, situated at the west end of the platforms, which were converted to half barriers in September 1992 at which time control passed to Chichester. The signal box here dates from 1902 and was erected at a time when the LBSCR was changing from contractor-built lever frames to home-built patterns. Rather than the familiar Stevens style of vertically standing levers, which dropped downwards when pulled off, the levers here leant backwards in the normal position. At the time of this view the gates were still worked by the traditional capstan wheel. In 1982 a number of 2 HAPs were permanently coupled together to form 4 CAPs (Coastway) sets, the driving motor vehicle cabs in the centre of the unit being decommissioned to reduce weight. The final HAPs were withdrawn from service in 1994/95 with unit No. 4311 preserved at the Electric Railway Museum at Baginton near Coventry.*   *Jeffery Grayer collection*

Guest Editorial

Welcome to issue 20 of The Southern Way which is actually the twenty first volume to appear in the series. In a break from tradition and to celebrate that event there is a guest in the editorial chair!

Let me commence with a reference to the view on this page, which is a photograph of the ex LB&SCR Stroudley "terrier" class A1x no (3)2636, photographed around the time of nationalisation at Newhaven by my former French teacher, Mr Derek Ives. This photograph has been in my possession for over 50 years. It is probably my favourite photograph of a steam engine, a thing of beauty.

If you are reading Southern Way then you will very likely value the artefacts, the people and the operations of the Southern Railway or BR(S) above others. The Southern was in many ways unique. You only have to consider it as a commuter railway in the London suburbs, as a long distance railway to the far West or as an operator of steam ships to observe that there is a rich vein of material which remains to be explored and recorded. We must be grateful for the Southern bias of Noodle books!

As a guest editor however, I propose to raise an issue which may be contentious and which may stray from the themes which Kevin proposed in the editorial in the preview volume, namely the issue of railway preservation. Now, there are magazines which cover the preservation scene and we should be grateful to the many volunteers who put so much time and effort into the preservation and operation of steam railways. But there is a matter which is being overlooked and that is honesty in the preservation, repair or restoration of artefacts and I particularly refer to those of the Southern Railway and its pre- grouping antecedents in which we have an interest.

The issue is the nature of the repair and restoration and the skill lies in mending with the minimum loss of historic fabric and so of romance and authenticity.

Restoration too often means work intended to restore the artefact to a perfect state. It may be the unnecessary renewal of worn features, or the hypothetical reconstruction of whole or missing elements. One must accept that railway vehicles were always repaired to a contemporary standard and that parts were renewed. Steam engines for instance need new boilers. But I do not believe it is appropriate to restore a working steam engine to an earlier hypothetical state, for that is a deception and devalues the genuine article.

That is where the frontispiece is relevant. "Fenchurch" is currently "restored" to appear as William Stroudley intended, an "A" class or later "A1", but it actually has I believe an A1x type boiler, so it is a hybrid. In the process it has lost that historical continuity which was its character and its value as a historic artefact. Whilst we should be grateful the veteran is still in steam, it is now an imposter, but how many people realise? How many care? It is after all very attractive in its current form. From a historical perspective, such as we seek within these pages, the deception must be a worry.

Alan Charles Moon.
Salisbury, Wiltshire. August 2012.

This editorial is a personal view and should not be taken as the opinion or policy of the publisher. The guest Editor is a Chartered Architect practicing in South Wiltshire.

Alan,

Thank you. I have no doubt there will be those who wish to comment, we welcome it. We intend to continue the 'Guest Editor' feature on occasions in the future, if you would like to feature please contact us.

Finally it is with regret that I must announce a rise in the cover price of 'Southern Way' from January 2013. We have held the price, notwithstanding extra pages in most issues, since Issue No 7 in July 2009. Postage and printing are the culprits. Consequently from No 21 the cover price will rise to £14.50. We are NOT changing the cover price of the back issues. Subscription renewals will be held at the old rate of £51.80 (UK) until the end of March 2013, we will also continue to send all our books post-free in the UK.. Thank you for your support.

*I will also say something rather special is planned for No 21....**including 120 pages.***

Kevin Robertson editorial@thesouthernway.co.uk

Above - LBSCR motor luggage van No. 10112 in original form as built in 1923. These rather unusual vehicles normally ran in the centre of a 5-coach rake of AC electric stock on services to Coulsdon and Wallington (hence the CW classification), providing the motive power and accommodation for luggage and the guard. As a consequence the staff referred to them as "milk vans", although it is doubtful if they ever carried this cargo. The driving positions at each end were normally used only for shunting purposes – the usual driving position was in the leading cab of the five-coach train. (really four passenger vehicles and a motor van.) Technically far superior to the ex-LSWR 600 volt outside third pick-up the overhead system was doomed after the Grouping – it was a Brighton idea after all, but the smaller mileage compared to the DC system and the far higher cost of installation all weighed against it. This van subsequently became 'gondola' 56265.　　　　O. J. Morris/SR

A Look at Southern Goods Brake Vans
Part 2 - Gondolas, Queen Mary's and Ploughs

Mike King

(Part 1 appeared in Issue No 18.)

In part one we looked at the ordinary four-wheeled 15- and 25-ton brake vans and their pre-Grouping ancestry – now it is the turn of the more specialised vehicles.

Once it was decided that provision of vacuum brakes on the four-wheelers was not an easy option, someone realised that the former LBSCR AC motor luggage vans might be put to good use as vacuum-fitted brakes for express services. 21 of these vans had been built in 1923/4 for the Brighton's "elevated electric" services to Coulsdon and Wallington (planned by the LBSCR but completed in the early days of the Southern). Once these routes had been converted to third rail DC operation in 1929 the vans had been stored at Streatham Hill pending a decision as to what to do with them. The Southern's management, ever loath to waste anything, had at first issued an order to rebuild them into bogie bolster wagons, but at only 42 ft over buffers they might have proved rather too short to be of much use – consequently little or nothing had been done to progress the conversions. Instead, in July 1933 an order was placed to convert just one van into a bogie goods brake – the result being no. 56263 (why not 56261, as this was the next vacant number in the series?), which emerged from Eastleigh works three months later. This proved highly satisfactory and no time was lost converting the remainder in similar fashion and these entered service between March 1934 and January 1935. They were allocated SR Diagram number 1580 and running numbers 56261/2/4-81, being officially described as "bogie goods brake vans for express service". Southern men, as we have seen, were adept at giving nicknames so these became known as "gondolas", perhaps because of their superior riding qualities. They all tared between 27 and 28 tons. Compared with the four-wheelers they were a dream – comfortable, spacious and unlike the pillboxes, rode well at any speed.

As ex-LBSCR rebuilds they were destined to be non-standard in a number of ways. This also resulted in both sides having a slightly different arrangement of windows (compare photographs) and they had the distinctive profile of carriage stock – even though they were steel-sheeted in place of the former typical Brighton timber panelling. The prototype van also differed in a few details from the others. Pressed steel lookouts were provided; these were recovered from suburban electric units as roof periscopes were then being fitted instead – reused in the Southern's usual thrifty manner – standard side duckets could not be provided as the vans were rather wider than other goods brakes. The original 8ft 9in wheelbase bogies were retained, minus of course the electrical equipment and this was probably the main reason for their early withdrawal in the late 1950s – this feature by then emphasising their non-standard nature. Five vans (nos. 56270/2/3/7/81) were transferred to the Civil Engineer's department in 1957 and lasted until at least 1964 on rail and ballast train workings. Just whether any were repainted in the then current departmental livery of black with yellow lettering is not known – most seem to have retained bauxite livery merely with the number prefixed DS and the letters E's added to denote ownership, together with a return to Redbridge Works instruction.

The success of these vans ensured that it was not long before more were required and a further batch of 25 was ordered in April 1935. These were to be new-build and were mounted on a shortened version of the carriage stock underframe and running on standard 8ft wheelbase bogies. Constructionally the bodywork was similar to the four-wheeled brake vans but extended to 24ft 6in long, bringing the veranda entrance almost over the bogie centre-lines – probably a safety consideration. Most vans had a timber-planked finish but some received steel-sheet side panels from new – many of the others were similarly modified in their later years. SR running numbers 56282-306 were

Opposite bottom - The prototype express goods brake van, No. 56263 to Diagram 1580 as outshopped in September 1933. There were slight detail differences between this van and the "production" batch – the most obvious being the lack of the inverted vee cutout in the sandboxes. The side lookouts came from suburban electric units, which were then being fitted with roof periscopes instead. The red ends to the veranda show up against the brown side panels but it is not so clear if the headstocks and buffer casings are also the same colour. Quite a contrast to a standard "pillbox".   *SR Official*

End view of van No. 56274 at Feltham on 31 March 1950, showing the different sandbox detail. The slope of the lid is also steeper. The greater width of the vehicle is apparent in this view. Livery was recorded not as SR brown with red ends but "dirty black". Make of that what you will.

A. E. West

allocated, along with Diagram 1550. This diagram number had already been issued to three ex-Diagram 1541 LSWR rebuilds for the Canterbury and Whitstable branch and was an almost unique duplication - presumably an error made in the carriage and wagon clerical department. The vans emerged from Ashford works (on underframes provided by Lancing) between May and August 1936, proving to be just as popular as the rebuilds. They may have been some of the last new construction to receive the large (18 inch) company initials as use of 4 inch lettering commenced in the same year. As usual they soon acquired a nickname - "Queen Marys" – the great liner carrying the same name had made her maiden voyage just as the first vans appeared and so was on everybody's minds at the time.

Both types were used indiscriminately on express goods services - mostly between London and the channel ports and between Nine Elms and Southampton, Dorchester and the West of England and would have been an unlikely sight on branch lines at that period. Rebuild 56278 was lost to enemy action in August 1943, while at least one other and two Diagram 1550's served with the army during the war. One conveyed the prime minister, Winston Churchill, on an inspection of long-range guns being used on the Martin Mill military railway near Dover.

After nationalisation, all 45 survivors were repainted from SR brown with red ends into BR fitted stock bauxite, but at least one was recorded in grey (still with red ends) in 1950. In contrast to the rebuilds, the Diagram 1580 vans were destined to have a long life under British

Railways and some have only recently been withdrawn from service. Six (nos. 56285//6/96/9/301/3) were equipped with Westinghouse brakes for Continental freight traffic between Hither Green and Dover in 1961 while most others have been air-piped in more recent times. By the 1970s they could be met with almost anywhere in the country – indeed at least two were allocated to the electrification works between Carlisle and Glasgow in 1974 – complete with yellow and black chevron painted ends. Others have seen various sector liveries and had sandboxes removed, while it is believed at least one was fully steel-sheeted, enclosing the open veranda ends. Quite a number are now in the hands of preservation societies and are much favoured for brake van rides – the author has travelled in van 56290 on a number of occasions on the Bluebell Railway. Van 56297 is now part of the national collection, restored to SR livery and based at York.

Three even more unusual brake vans were completed in 1938 specifically for the Folkestone Harbour branch. This steeply graded line (up to 1 in 30) had used four, latterly three, ex-SER incline or bank brake vehicles since the 1860s and by the mid-1930s these were overdue for replacement. Diagram 1561 (the diagram number that perhaps should have been allocated to the 1928 "pillboxes") was issued, together with running numbers 55180-2; appropriately just ahead of the number block allocated to former SECR brakes. The "vans" were mounted on former LBSCR B2X tender underframes – themselves already second-hand as they had originally been built for "Horsham

The other side of a Diagram 1580 van showing the slightly different window/droplight arrangement found on all 21 vans. No. 56264, photographed sometime in the 1930s. The steeper slope of the sandbox top is also visible. When new this carried the word "sand" but this does not seem to have been perpetuated on later repaintings.   *Authors Collection*

Goods" C3 0-6-0s. They were more an amalgamation of standard parts rather than a design and aesthetics do not seem to have played much of a part in their appearance – just look at the photograph. They were formed partly of an enclosed portion, with standard "pillbox" lookouts on each side and an open section with drop flap sides that allowed them to be used to convey equipment and personnel to and from Folkestone Warren, which was separated from Folkestone Junction by Martello tunnel and at that time did not have any road access. Apart from a wartime spell on the Martin Mill military railway, they seldom ventured further than Ashford works for overhaul. The author came to know the Folkestone Harbour branch from 1956 and never saw the vans used – they were parked up in a siding and seldom moved. Local opinion was that they were ineffective as

brake vans ("pillboxes" or BR vans were used instead) but perhaps had they retained all six tender wheels with brakes on all of them, they might have performed better. Withdrawal occurred in 1969 – a special traffic stencil dated 24th September 1969 records that all three were to be forwarded from Folkestone Junction to Acton on that date, thence to Cardiff for scrapping. By contrast the fourth ancient ex-SER bank brake van was transferred away to the Topsham Quay branch in Devon following a runaway accident about 1925 and lasted almost until the branch closed in 1953 – quite possibly making it the longest-lived SR wagon of its era.

The final design of traffic department brake van to be considered is the RCH vehicle. Despite the early adoption of common user policies for many wagons, goods

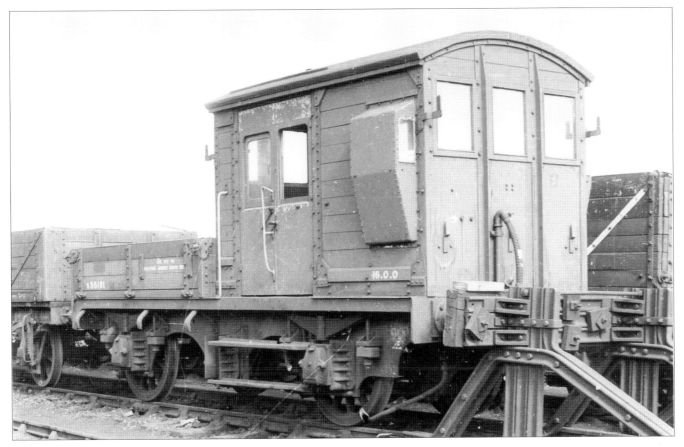

Opposite top - *The new-build version of bogie brake van to Diagram 1550. Van 56302 is seen at Southampton Docks soon after construction in August 1936. This is a fully planked example. Note the still pristine finish, disfigured only by the chalked road numbers on the end – an indication that the vehicle has probably been over Feltham humps several times – this being the method of indicating to the hump signal cabin which road to send the van into.* F. Foote

Opposite bottom - *A part steel-sheeted van, no. S56300 in bauxite livery at Axminster on a rather wet 21st July 1960. This shows the opposite side – without the vacuum pipe along the solebar. Note that there is a lamp iron inside the veranda end on which to store tail lamps when not required. A Maunsell cattle wagon stands beyond.* A. E. West

Above - *Folkestone Harbour brake tender S55181, parked (as usual) against the buffer stops at Folkestone Junction some time in the early 1950s. Bauxite livery with the inscription "For use on Folkestone Harbour branch only" on the open dropside portion. Despite officially being recorded as 15-ton vehicles, all three tared not less than 16 tons. Standard duckets, doors, handrails and probably other parts, too. The enclosed van section always faced the harbour (ie. down) direction.*
Authors Collection

The RCH brake van, No. S56060, at Westerham on 5 May 1956 – possibly still in SR brown livery. The wagon plate records the construction date as Derby, 1943 – three years before delivery to the Southern Railway, so presumably all four vans were retained as LMS stock during this time, running numbers being in the series 731742-46. The sand box is on the end platform over the headstock with the control mechanism passing vertically up the veranda end and under the roof to the control handle inside the cabin. The italic lettering instructs that the van was "Not to work between Tonbridge and West St Leonards via Battle. The tare weight is exactly 20 tons – the other big four companies did not agree that the extra 5 tons tare weight was necessary – but they were more often using motive power designed specifically for goods train haulage. P. Coutanche

brake vans were not considered in this category until 1942 – old habits died hard with most pre-Grouping brake vans staying on their home territory far more than other goods vehicles. It was really only the exigencies of World War Two that made any great difference to this state of affairs. In 1943, following consultation with each of the big four companies and the Railway Clearing House, the LMS built four vans (one for each company) with a view to getting universal agreement on design matters. The SR van was duly received, possibly as late as 1946, and was allocated Diagram number 1570 and running number 56060. A few modifications were made on receipt; including the fitting of veranda gates and SR lamp brackets and it then joined the general pool of standard 20/25 ton vans, being given no special treatment. Photographs show the van as far apart as Exeter and Dover and it ended its days as a "local use" van between Dover Marine and Dover Priory about 1967. The design owed little to the "pillboxes" and was probably more akin to LNER vehicles than any other. Interestingly, the GWR van (no. 35927) ended up marked "Frome

R.U." (restricted use) while the LNER van (no. 260948) worked similarly at North Tyneside Quay, perhaps leaving only the LMS vehicle (no. 731742) in general use.

We now come to ballast brake vans. Not only were these designed to provide braking power but in many instances doubled up as riding vans to carry the permanent way staff to and from site – quite often inaccessible by other means of transport at night or at weekends – or as ballast ploughs used to spread the stone already laid by the hopper wagons. In Southern days they were finished in red oxide livery with slightly brighter red ends while after 1948 they carried whatever Civil Engineering department livery was in vogue – black, olive green or "Dutch" yellow and grey if they lasted long enough.

In 1923 the Southern inherited 73 vehicles classified as ballast brakes and allocated to the Civil Engineer – not that use of traffic department brakes for ballasting work was unknown. Many were already fairly elderly and some ex-LBSCR Stroudley examples were former traffic department cast-offs anyway. Only seven

The LBSCR 20-ton ballast brake van design of 1915. No. S62835 (ex-LBSCR No. 328) is seen at its home depot of Three Bridges on 30 April 1950, in what is probably SR red oxide livery. The other side is identical, ie. the doors are at diagonally opposite corners. These vans provided riding as well as guard's accommodation.

D. Cullum/The Lens of Sutton Association

could be described as modern; six LBSCR 6-wheelers built in 1915 and a solitary SECR ballast plough dating from a year earlier. Predictably, the LBSCR vans found little favour under the new CME, leaving the SECR design to be perpetuated by the Southern. Ex-SECR no. 6330/SR no. 62523 (to SR Diagram 1748) was a long-wheelbase 20-ton vehicle having two sets of ploughs contained within the wheelbase to facilitate ballast spreading in either direction. It had originally been ordered in 1910 along with a train of seven 4-wheeled ballast hopper wagons. The hoppers were actually built in 1911 by the Leeds Forge Company but for some reason the brake van was deferred, only to be considered again two years later as its construction was authorised and signed off by Harry Wainwright on 16th September 1912. Construction clearly did not go ahead immediately, as the van failed to appear from Ashford works until two years later. By this time Maunsell and Lynes were in charge, but it is unclear whether the design originated with Wainwright or with the two latter gentlemen. Nothing on general arrangement drawings 3393 and 3394 (dated 1910 by numerical sequence, although the design might hail from later) indicate revisions prior to the construction of another batch in late Southern days, of which more anon. What is known is that van 6330 was booked out from Ashford works in June 1914 at a recorded cost of £545 – quite a lot more than other brake vans of the period. It must have worked with the 1911 hoppers for a time, as it was not until 1915 that a further train of seven hoppers (of an improved design) was completed, again by the Leeds Forge Company.

Maunsell and Lynes clearly found the van useful, as three more were built by Charles Roberts & Company in 1932, SR numbers being 62030-32, following on from the 40-ton bogie hoppers ordered from Metropolitan three years earlier. These ploughs followed the SECR prototype in all but minor details and were allocated the same diagram

number (1748). Apart from the conversion of LBSCR Diagram 1576/1760 ballast brakes, here matters rested until 1945 when a further batch of bogie ballast hoppers was ordered, bringing the total on the Southern to 87 (20 ex-LSWR bogies and the rest to SR Diagrams 1772/4/5). It was clearly felt that more ploughs were needed and eight more, SR Nos. 62857-64 to Diagram 1749, were ordered in 1945. These finally appeared in April 1949 carrying BR black livery with yellow lettering. From the evidence of notes on the original SECR general arrangement drawings, these were used again with only minor revisions. The arrival of these allowed the final withdrawal of a few really ancient ex-SER ballast brake vans, the underframes of some of which dated from as far back as 1865. All 12 plough vans remained in use into the 1980s: however the proximity of the live rail often rendered them useless as ploughs in their later years despite modifications to the shape of the ploughs to try to overcome this. Even the SECR prototype of 1914 managed to put in 75 years service, finally being withdrawn in 1989. Since the 1970s no. 62523 had been noted at locations as widely scattered as Par and Nottingham. It has now been preserved by the Midland Railway Trust at Butterley. Some of the others lasted equally as long and several are now in the hands of preservations societies – still fulfilling the function for which they were designed.

Returning to the early years of the Southern Railway, the next significant event occurred on the evening of 24th August 1927, when "River" class tank no. A800 was derailed at speed near Sevenoaks. Whilst no real blame could be placed on the locomotive, it showed up the deficiencies in the SECR's trackwork; in particular the ballast, which was made up mainly of Dungeness shingle. As a precaution and probably a damage limitation exercise, all 21 "River" tanks were immediately withdrawn from traffic and in due course rebuilt as nameless 2-6-0 tender locomotives – a form that would allow them to continue to

Above - Rebuilt Panter Diagram 1576 brake van No. S62851, now to Diagram 1760, at Ashford on 8 July 1951, in red oxide livery. The lettering states "Engr's Dept Eastern Division. Ballast train No. 1. Return to Ashford Kent". The enclosed right-hand end now provides P/Way staff riding accommodation while the guard occupies the nearer end of the vehicle, where the handbrake remains on the open veranda end. Note the inset side sheeting between the windows – allowing the lamp irons also to be inset to clear the Tonbridge-Hastings line gauge but still be visible to enginemen at the front of the train. A. E. West

Opposite top - Ballast plough brake van No. 62030 at Tonbridge on 2 August 1932, showing the non-standard company lettering applied by Charles Roberts & Company. These three vans (62030-32) were practically identical to the SECR prototype and were allocated the same diagram number - 1748. The only really obvious detail differences were buffers and roof vents.

H. F. Wheeller

work faultlessly for up to 38 years. The result as far as the Civil Engineer was concerned was an urgent programme of track and ballast renewal, not just on the South Eastern but also on the Brighton line as well, immediately requiring a number of additional ballast wagons and brake vans. The requirement for ballast wagons was quickly met by an order for 60 dropside vehicles from Birmingham RCW Co but for brake vans four ancient LCDR 4-wheeled coaches were hastily converted from withdrawn stock, followed by seven of A.H. Panter's LBSCR brake vans to Diagram 1576. These were some of the most modern brake vans on the Brighton section but their lack of side lookouts may have been the reason for their selection – this omission had already led to disfavour by some goods guards while relatively little modification would be needed to enable them to run down the restricted Tonbridge-Hastings line – one of those clearly requiring major track relaying. The four

LCDR coaches, SR numbers 62524-7, received no SR diagram number (perhaps their life was expected to be short, yet in the event all four put in at least 20 years service!) while the LBSCR rebuilds became Diagram 1760 and a further 10 were similarly rebuilt in 1937, some running into the 1980s in this form, considerably outlasting any of the originals. SR numbers of these were 62840-56.

One other possible explanation for the choice of Diagram 1576 for conversion was that they were large enough to provide both guard's and riding accommodation – one end veranda being enclosed and converted into the permanent way staff compartment. All were vacuum-fitted on conversion. Perhaps for the same reason the final 10 Southern Region conversions of 1953 utilised former SECR "dance halls" in exactly the same way. These were numbers 55476/82//6/9/92-4/9, 55502/8 from Diagram 1560. All retained their former traffic department numbers but were

This page, bottom - *1949-built Ashford plough brake no. DS62857 to Diagram 1749 – again there were few differences from the earlier vehicles but no oil lamps were provided and the window detail was triflingly changed. Internally the control wheels were altered slightly. The van now carries BR olive green livery and the code name "Shark". The location is Meldon Quarry sidings on 15 May 1965. End steps were not fitted to these vans – because no oil lamps were provided there was no need to access the roof.*

A. E. West

reallocated to SR Diagram 1761. Like their rebuilt LBSCR counterparts, these too served until at least the 1980s – both on and off the Southern Region. Again, all were vacuum-braked on conversion to enable them to work with the ballast hoppers and other Engineer's Department stock, while some were later air-piped in addition.

After this quite a number of standard "pillboxes" and "dance halls" were transferred unmodified to the Engineer's stock, with nothing more than the addition of the departmental prefix "DS" ahead of the traffic department running numbers, together with a repaint into the then current ED livery. Some of these were later air-piped and remained in service until recent years and are very often those now in the hands of the preservation societies, thanks to their longevity in Engineer's stock. Indeed, one railwayman once remarked to me that the Southern Region's rolling stock staff were running their own preservation society within the departmental stock! Whatever the truth or otherwise of that statement, it certainly emphasised the sound nature of the design and construction of the vehicles concerned.

Above - *The final ballast brake van conversions were the ten rebuilt "dance halls" to Diagram 1761, dating from 1953. This is No. DS55486 at East Grinstead High Level on 5 October 1969 – probably there in connection with demolition works and wearing olive green livery. The Permanent Way riding accommodation is at the left-hand end and the general similarity with the ex-LBSCR Diagram 1760 conversions is apparent. However, no width reduction measures were made for the lamp irons, yet the vans were not restricted from travelling on the Hastings direct line. Probably the Chief Civil Engineer's attitude had changed since the days of the Sevenoaks derailment, relations havings mellowed considerably since then. Appropriately as the last illustration it is also the most recent photograph used in these two articles.* E. R. Kemp

Opposite bottom - *At the other extreme is former LCDR ballast brake van conversion 62525 of October 1927, photographed shortly after the end of World War Two and labelled 'Eastern Division Ashford Kent - Ballast Train No. 1', so its replacement was clearly LBSCR brake 62851, seen on page 14. The coach was stripped internally and equipped with a stove and handbrake, with probably makeshift bench seating all round. Notice that only the four corner doors remain accessible. Dimensions were 25ft long by 8ft wide and the coach originally dates from 1884. This vehicle and no. 62527 were ex-5 compartment thirds while nos. 62524/26 were ex-3 compartment brakes and all had done a stint on hop pickers trains before withdrawal from passenger traffic. Even as passenger coaches they had been oil-lit!*

The Lens of Sutton Association

Above - A close-up view of the plough under van 62032 at Meldon Quarry, also on 15th May 1965. This shows it in the normal or raised position. Also visible is the Charles Roberts works plate and the SR number plate.   A E West

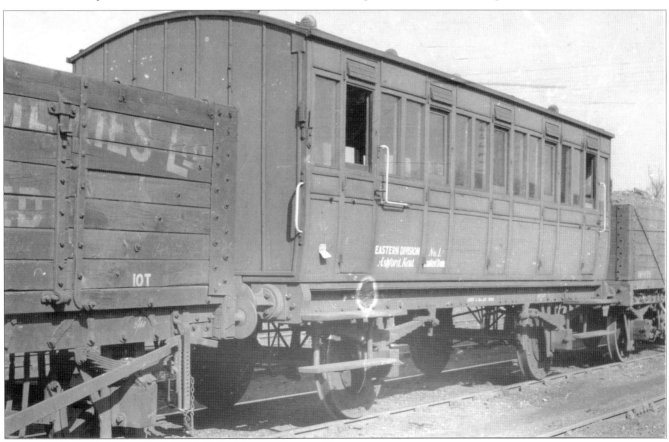

Southern Railwaymen

Alan Postlethwaite

Ashurst Junction (opposite page) had an LB&SCR gabled signal box located between two key junctions on the Brighton's secondary network: Up to Oxted or East Grinstead; and Down to Tunbridge Wells West or Eridge. Photographed in 1963, John Fuller is neatly turned out, looking as spotless as his lever frame and instrument shelf. The clock is lit by an electric lamp with an oil lamp as standby. The staff instrument was for the single-track line to East Grinstead. The other lines were double-track.
John Fuller **(left)** joined BR in 1953 as a porter/ shunter at Eridge. He became a relief signalman at Birch End Junction and Ashurst Junction, then signalman at East Grinstead, Hurst Green, Lingfield and Uckfield. He retired in 1985 and was 88 in early 2010.

Ryde St Johns Road (above) had the largest signal box on the Isle of Wight. The line southwards was double-track in summer and two single tracks in winter. The box was of SE&CR design, transferred in 1928 from Waterloo Junction, 17 years after the link to the L&SWR was lifted. Photographed in 1960, Dick Russell was one of two railway brothers. The tidiness of his box is apparent, from the linoleum and tool boxes to the fire buckets, coats, loudhailer and kettle on the stove.

Track maintenance workers were known as linemen - not to be confused with the phrase 'linesman' who looked after signal and telegraph electrical equipment. As well as repairing track, they cut lineside trees, undergrowth and grass, 'firing' it every few years. Their scythes and sickles look formidable. In these portraits, hats are a mix of trilby, beret and 'cheese-cutter'. Four are wearing bib-and-brace overalls, some with jackets. Trousers were generally tied at the ankles to guard against rats **Near Daggons Road** in 1963 are (L to R) A. Edsall, Jack Mussell and Frank King. Of the six linesmen featured across these pages, Jack Mussell was the last survivor, passing away in 1995. He was well-known locally as a bell-ringer

Between Wareham and Wool in 1963 are (L to R) Stan Smith, Arthur 'Art' Welsh and Leo 'Len' Burden. Wearing a three-piece suit, sub-Inspector Burden was in charge of the Poole and Wareham gangs. Starting work in 1923 at the age of twenty, he became a sub-ganger in 1928 in charge of five men including his own father. His grandfather also worked on this line, serving for fifty years bar ten days. This gang recalled a linesman called Stevens who found a wooden bridge washed away near here. After running to Wool, he knocked out the 'signal pin' to make it inoperable, just in time to prevent the next train from starting. His reward was a set of furniture which he went to London to receive.

The EPB Story Part 1 - An Introduction

David Monk-Steel

Development of South London Suburbia

During the Nineteenth Century London grew in area and population at an astonishing rate. In 1841 the population of Greater London was 290,000 but by 1901, sixty years later, it had increased sevenfold to 2,050,000.

Better health, employment opportunities and improvement in life expectancy had all contributed to this expansion. London was a magnet to people from all parts of the United Kingdom but the indigenous Londoners also prospered and these extra people needed somewhere to live. The City and Central London were either too congested or too expensive for most people who looked further out for suitable homes. The people from the increasing numbers of 'Middle Classes' tended to move out of London first. They could afford to buy the large villas being built round about the villages near London and the cost of travel to their place of business daily, either by private vehicle or by the new 'buses, all of which were horse-drawn. As soon as their lines were opened, the newly formed railway companies also started to cater for this market. Stations opened in the new suburbs to tap into this business traveller market. Despite efforts by Parliament, railway fares tended to be too high to encourage the ordinary working man to seek a suburban lifestyle at that time, but the expanding 'Middle Class' sought out the new suburbs and with it the trains as a vital link between home and office.

The Development of a Railway Network

The Southern Railway and its successor the Southern Region of British Railways, which will mainly concern us later, held a virtual monopoly of South London and the counties of Kent, Surrey, Sussex, Hampshire and Dorset. It was created out of four of the larger pre-grouping concerns located south of the River Thames, namely the South Eastern Railway, the London Chatham & Dover Railway, (who had been jointly managed by the South Eastern & Chatham Managing Committee since 1898), the London, Brighton & South Coast Railway and the London & South Western Railway.

Each line had distinct operating areas in the London Suburbs, and distinct London termini. In brief these were.

The **London and South Western Railway** operated exclusively from Waterloo on the south bank of the River Thames serving West Surrey, including the towns of Richmond, Kingston upon Thames, Wimbledon, Surbiton, Guildford, Staines, Windsor and Reading. It also had main lines to Southampton, Portsmouth, and numerous places in the west of England.

The **London, Brighton and South Coast Railway** which served East Surrey including Mitcham, Sutton, Croydon, Epsom, Dorking and Redhill, from two stations, London Bridge near to Southwark Cathedral, for City-bound travellers, and Victoria, across the river in Pimlico, serving the West End. This railway also served the South Coast from Hastings and Brighton in Sussex to Havant and Portsmouth in Hampshire.

The **London, Chatham and Dover Railway** had a terminus at Victoria alongside the 'Brighton' one, and served Sydenham, Bromley, Orpington and Swanley. It also linked up across London with the Great Northern and Midland Railways via Blackfriars, and had a terminus serving the City of London off this line near St. Paul's Cathedral on Ludgate Hill. It had its origins in East Kent, centred upon Faversham, and operated lines to Dover, Ramsgate and Ashford via Maidstone.

Its arch rival, the **South Eastern Railway** had stations for the West End at Charing Cross in the Strand, and at Cannon Street also near St. Paul's, but served Greenwich, Woolwich, Dartford, Bromley, Orpington, Sidcup and Eltham. It had arrived on the scene before the Chatham Company, having its origins in the Canterbury and Whitstable Railway opened in 1830 and the London and Greenwich Railway opened in 1836. It operated to Ramsgate, Dover and Hastings, but it reached these places by a circuitous route through Tonbridge.

All four companies had well established suburban networks before the end of the century.

Competition from Street Tramways

Trams were cheaper and therefore brought travel advantages to the working class who were able to move away from Central London.

Horse tramways were operating from Clapham, Brixton, New Cross and Greenwich since the early 1870s, but the purchase of these lines by the London County Council, and subsequently their electrification spelt trouble for the main line railways, whose reputation for customer service was very poor. Through electric tram car routes were operating to central London from Putney (January 1912), Tooting (May 1903), Streatham (June 1904), West Norwood

Class 415/1, 4EPB N0 5049, and class 416/3 2EPB No. 5714 form the 10.51 am Cannon Street, Sidcup, Chislehurst service near Mottingham on 22 August 1979.
Brian Morrison

(May 1909), Forest Hill (December 1908), Catford (June 1906), Lewisham (January 1906), Eltham - Lee Green (May 1907) and Woolwich (April 1911). Towns like Croydon had their own tram systems, but until these were physically connected to the London County Council Tramways in the 1920s passengers would require least one change of vehicle to make a through journey to London. In some areas too, the new Underground electric railways were strong competitors to the main line railways, but south of the River Thames their influence was significantly less than that north of it. By the end of the nineteenth century electric trams were also starting to eat into the railway's share of the middle class market, and before the Great War all the principal railway companies who served London were forced to consider electrification to counter tramway competition.

The London & South Western and London, Brighton and South Coast Railways led the way, electrifying their inner suburban services, and realising the benefits, continued to extend it into the 'leafy suburbs' of Wimbledon, Shepperton, Croydon and Sutton. This restored their competitive 'edge' and brought increased revenues to the railways. It also stimulated further speculative suburban building development, which brought its own problems by increasing demand.

In 1923 the Railways were grouped into the 'Big Four' (Southern, London Midland and Scottish, London and North Eastern and Great Western Railways). Simultaneously there was significant suburban development taking place in the counties of Kent and Surrey. This was further encouraged by political stimulus to the house building industry to counter the problems of unemployment that was afflicting the United Kingdom at the time.

New private housing tended to be sought by the middle class many of whom worked in the City and West End. The working class population still tended to live close to their work, and the tram (and later the trolleybus which replaced it) was usually their chosen mode of transport. Dockland, and the new industrial estates of the period were often remote from the railway network in any case.

Competition with the Tube

Unlike the companies who operated train services in north and west London the constituents of the Southern were relatively free of tube incursions. The exceptions were the City & South London line to Elephant & Castle and eventually to Morden, and the Metropolitan District between Brentford and Hounslow, (later to incorporate extensions of the Piccadilly Line), and its lines to Richmond and Wimbledon.

Expansion continues

Between 1901 and 1939 Greater London population more than doubled to 4,715,000. The inner areas had been fully exploited by this time, and therefore estates were built further out into Kent and Surrey. Demand for housing was changing: the large family villa of Victorian and Edwardian eras requiring domestic servants to operate successfully was no longer fashionable, and the easy to run semi-detached house became the 'ideal' home. These large estates of small suburban 'semis' were heavily criticised by the architectural 'intelligentsia' at the time.

There is considerable argument as to whether the railways caused suburban growth or were a symptom of it. This is not the place to debate that further but it is certain that without a network of lines from Kent and Surrey into the heart of the Capital the establishment of Suburban London would have been extremely difficult. The following figures illustrate how certain places grew after the coming of the railway in the late Nineteenth Century and then how that growth accelerated after electrification in the late Nineteen Twenties.

This expansion was set to continue unchecked (save for two World Wars) until 1945. At that time the London Suburban area was defined as the area enclosed by and including, Staines, Shepperton, Chertsey, Weybridge, Cobham, Leatherhead, Epsom, Caterham, New Addington, Hayes (Kent), Orpington, Swanley and Dartford, although most of these places were well outside the London County Council boundaries, and did not eventually become part of Greater London.

This area was well served by the railway network and few people lived more than a mile and a half from a railway station, e.g. 30 minutes walk or ten minutes on the 'bus.

Capacity problems on the Southern approaches to London

Peak hour operation has capacity problems that are very difficult to solve. There could never be enough lines linking the termini to the suburbs to handle the number of trains required for just a few hours per day. Land was expensive and the demolition of property in the central area was very

Population				
Year	1901	1921	1931	1939
Bexley (including Bexleyheath)	15,000	21104	32626	80110
Carshalton	6700	14023	28586	59510
Epsom & Ewell	10900	18803	35228	62690
Malden & Coombe	6200	14503	23350	39930

Rush hour at Victoria, 12 August 1949. Save for the fashions, the volume of passengers changed little over the decades.

unpopular. The railway companies made the best of it but the legacy even to the present day is a congested and inadequate infrastructure. On the South Eastern Railway's approach to Charing Cross and Cannon Street there were five SE tracks approaching London Bridge from the east, and six platform lines through the station, but these funnelled down into four lines from there through Borough Market Junction towards Cannon Street. Added to this the London Brighton and South Coast Railway terminated at London Bridge decanting passengers from their trains either to try to join South Eastern trains, or to walk in large procession across the Thames on London Bridge itself. This problem has never been adequately solved to this day although new Underground railway facilities in recent years are helping.

Early electrification schemes

The Southern Electric system grew from the roots put down originally by the London and South Western Railway in 1913. The first electric services ran on 25th October 1915, to Wimbledon via East Putney, and subsequently that company gradually extended its electric services until virtually all suburban lines in South West London and North West Surrey were electrified. Steam operations continued on a few routes, and for goods and long distance passenger for a further half-century.

The London and South Western Railway chose the third-rail system popular in the United States that used low tension 'continuous' or Direct Current, for cheapness and simplicity. This system was compatible with the newly-electrified Metropolitan District Railway, over whose tracks the London and South Western Railway operated in parts of West London. The officers of the Southern Railway, many of who came from the former London and South Western Railway, advocated that system of electric operation for future extensions.

The London Brighton and South Coast Railway had used High Tension Alternating Current supply to its electric trains introduced on 1st December 1909 to South London and North East Surrey, a full four years earlier than the London & South Western. It had managed to complete the electrification of the South London line between Victoria and London Bridge and routes to Norwood, West

THREE NEW ELECTRIC EXTENSIONS
WINDSOR·WRAYSBURY·DATCHET
·STAINES·ASHFORD·
1 FELTHAM·WATERLOO
TRAINS EVERY HALF HOUR
(Every 20 Mins: during Business rush)

GRAVESEND·GREENHITHE·
NORTHFLEET·DARTFORD
2 LONDON FOUR TRAINS PER HOUR

WEST CROYDON AND WIMBLEDON
3 ····VIA MITCHAM····
:: TRAINS EVERY HALF HOUR ::

MORE SPEED MORE TRAINS

FROM **6** JULY

SOUTHERN ELECTRIC

their differences and formed a working union in 1898), the London Brighton and South Coast Railway and London and South Western Railway were amalgamated with a number of smaller concerns in southern England to create the Southern Railway company. The Southern Railway became popularly associated with rush hour business trains, electrification, and seaside traffic. It was a passenger railway first and foremost serving the prosperous south of England where the effect of the economic troubles of the 1920s and 1930s were perhaps weathered far more effectively than elsewhere in Britain. Throughout its existence the Southern invariably paid its shareholders a dividend, albeit a very small one.

The Southern did not always have its own way. Challenges continued to come from tramways on the inner London suburban systems, and from motor omnibuses in more rural districts, but most importantly for this story, restricted terminal capacity in central London and the high cost of expansion in inner London were a constant hindrance. Only Waterloo station, rebuilt in the immediate post-war period by the London and South Western, was large enough for the purpose, and this station was half a mile or more from the City of London, and the wrong side of the Thames, where the large proportion of business travellers wished to go. True, there was 'the Drain' as the Waterloo and City Railway was known, but this entailed a complex interchange on more than one level.

In the London area the lines of route were divided administratively in much the same way as the former owning companies: thus these became London West, London Central and London East sections. Each served distinct terminals and preserved a good deal of the pre-grouping operating and rolling stock practices, at least for the first few years. For simplicity it was usual to refer to them as 'Western', 'Central' and 'Eastern' sections.

The Southern starts work on electrifying and modernising

Work started on further electrification by the Southern Railway included extensions to the former London and South Western Railway's system, to Dorking and Guildford, and the first schemes over lines of the former London Chatham and Dover Railway to Crystal Palace High Level, and to Orpington (ex-SER) serving the London termini of Victoria, Holborn Viaduct and Blackfriars. Services commenced on the 12th July 1925.

The Charing Cross and Cannon Street group of lines, formerly owned by the South Eastern Railway followed progressively in 1926, and brought electric trains to Dartford, Bromley North, Addiscombe and Hayes as well as providing an alternative route to Orpington.

Further Increase in capacity on the Eastern approaches

The electrification of the core suburban services of the former South Eastern Railway and London Chatham and

Croydon and Sutton before Grouping, but apart from a short extension to Coulsdon North completed by the Southern Railway, it was not adopted and in 1928 all the former A.C. lines were converted to D.C. operation.

The other major constituents of the Southern Railway had not started to electrify their suburban network, although they had identified an urgent need, especially as the termini at Charing Cross and Cannon Street and the lines serving South East London and Kent, were severely congested and difficult to operate. Plans had been made for a four-rail system but work had not started in earnest when the Great War broke out and the railways found themselves in the fore-front of demand to move men and materiel to the battlefields of France and Belgium, which was clearly not a good time to embark on a major renewal of infrastructure.

The Southern Railway takes over

The railways of Great Britain were grouped by Act of Parliament in 1923. The South Eastern Railway, London, Chatham and Dover Railway (both of whom had settled

Western Section electric. Windsor & Eton Riverside, with S1873, 1 December 1951.

The Lens of Sutton collection

Dover Railway systems into Charing Cross, Cannon Street, Victoria and Holborn Viaduct (St. Paul's) were completed by the Southern Railway in 1926. Many of the capacity problems experienced by those railways were temporarily solved by: -

- re-allocating the lines between North Kent East Junction and London Bridge,
- re-allocating the lines between Cannon Street and Charing Cross,
- re-modelling the approaches to Cannon Street and Charing Cross
- introduction of power-operated points and signalling with coloured-light four-aspect signals (a very early application), controlled from Blackfriars, Holborn Viaduct, Elephant & Castle, Charing Cross, Cannon Street, Metropolitan Junction, Borough Market Junction, London Bridge, North Kent East Junction, St. Johns, and Parks Bridge Junction signalboxes and the abolition of all others in that area
- revised siding arrangements and new country area stabling for the electric trains at Orpington, Addiscombe and Slade Green.[1]

The outer limits of the south-eastern suburban area have been generally defined as Dartford, Orpington, Bromley North, Hayes, Addiscombe and Crystal Palace (High Level), but in 1930 the lines to Gravesend, and Sevenoaks (by both Dunton Green and Otford) were added, and in 1935 the route from Woodside to Sanderstead was also energised together with a new link line between Lewisham and Nunhead.

As a general rule the former South Eastern Railway and London Chatham and Dover Railway routes were operated as discrete services, meeting only at Orpington, although the Lewisham to Nunhead link did give additional travel opportunities from North Kent to Holborn Viaduct and Blackfriars, it didn't really develop as had been intended, and was limited to a handful of peak period trains. These few always seemed to have more in common with the London Chatham and Dover Railway services than the South Eastern Railway's in any case.

Some benefits of electrification

Electrification in 1926 brought some relief, by removing the need for light engine and a significant proportion of empty coaching stock movements, together with the benefits of modern power-operated signalling but the underlying real capacity restraints were not solved, and the intrinsic defects in infrastructure lay in wait for future generations to solve. (It is still waiting!).

Further Electrification of the Western Section

The former London and South Western Railway's lines had already demonstrated the advantages of electrification and it was therefore inevitable that the Southern should wish to extend it. Having completed electrification to Guildford and Dorking, the Southern then started filling in the gaps and taking the third rail to outer suburban districts.

Conversion and extension to the Central Section

With DC third-rail finally established as company policy the London Brighton and South Coast Railway's A.C. overhead wire system was out of favour, and almost as soon as the final extension of the wire to Coulsdon was complete a start was made to introduce third-rail and progressively abandon wires. The wires had never existed between Bermondsey and Norwood so apart from Tulse Hill and South London services most suburban trains into London Bridge were still steam-hauled. To get third rail to Caterham and Tattenham Corner the line from London Bridge via Forest Hill was electrified in 1928, and then a start was made on straight replacement of the A.C. The Brighton main line followed in 1933 and that took the Southern into a higher league of electric railways. No longer did it handle just suburban traffic but prestige customers and in Pullman cars too, but this story is somewhat outside our present discussions.

Suburban Housing Expansion

As suburban expansion continued in the late 1920s & early 1930s, and new estates sprang up all round London, more trains were needed to handle the increased number of passengers wishing to travel in the peaks, especially on the Eastern section. Given the severe economic recession which was affecting the country at the time the Southern Railway had exercised remarkable ingenuity to carry out modernisation at low cost. They built 'new' rolling stock out of the old steam coaches using the old 'five-a-side' wooden bodies, usually fitted on to new 62' underframes. Only a handful of completely new carriages were built. A more detailed description of the Southern Railway electric rolling stock will follow in the next instalment.

Continuing problems of over-crowding

New stations appeared between Eltham and Welling on the Bexleyheath line, and between Sidcup and Bexley on the Dartford Loop. Sleepy rural stations like Barnehurst and Woodside suddenly found that they were the focus mornings and evenings for hundreds of new passengers. The problems of capacity returned with a vengeance as the following table shows.

At the outbreak of World War Two, in September 1939, the Southern Railway was moving about 125,000 workers into London every morning, and a similar number home each night.

TO BE CONTINUED.

1. The name 'Slades Green' was in use until the 1950s.

	Blackfriars & Holborn Viaduct	Cannon Street	Charing Cross	London Bridge	Victoria	Waterloo East	Waterloo Main Line
Passengers arriving Peak-Hour: Monday-Friday							
1925	6486	11303	5120	Not recorded	10230	Not recorded	Not recorded
1926	8557	10513	5369	19247	11701	623	16887
1927	7344	10039	5244	18894	10207	643	15170
1928	7718	10182	6529	18893	10318	598	19467
1929	8698	13515	6934	25469	12893	1044	16618
1930	11197	15954	10160	27554	15003	1343	20845
1931	10319	13905	10685	25212	15145	1416	19165
1932	11050	13508	9319	25158	13770	1363	19294
1933	10109	15084	11551	25531	13762	1635	19090
1934	11095	14661	13043	27317	14001	1543	19150
1935	11729	16574	14456	26496	15143	1698	22307
1936	13718	16443	17910	28827	16065	1845	20154
1937	14892	18936	17413	29489	17215	1922	23638
1938	13671	18135	17034	31260	16398	2184	24296

Source, Southern Railway official terminus census, taken each February.

Above - Borough Market Junction, May 1966, 4EPB set No. 5218.

Right - 4EPB set No. 5020 at Wimbledon.
          P J Sharpe.

SOUTHERN PRIVATE OWNERS. Never as prolific as on other railways, the southern area still played host to numerous private owner wagons, as well as receiving supplies in colliery based wagons. In response to numerous requests we present a few examples - no details we regret, but a picture does tell a thousand words!

Roger Carpenter / The Lens of Sutton collection

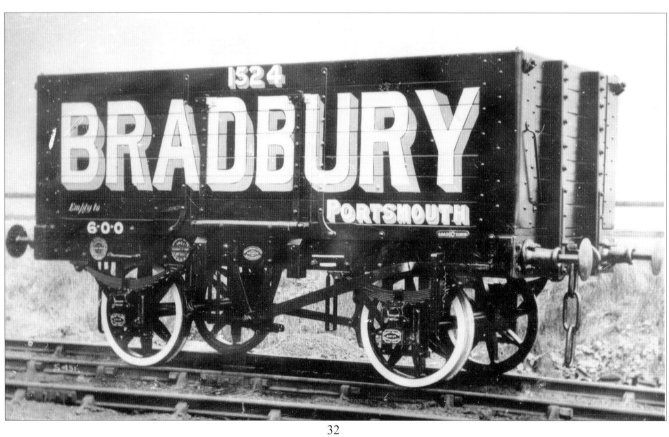

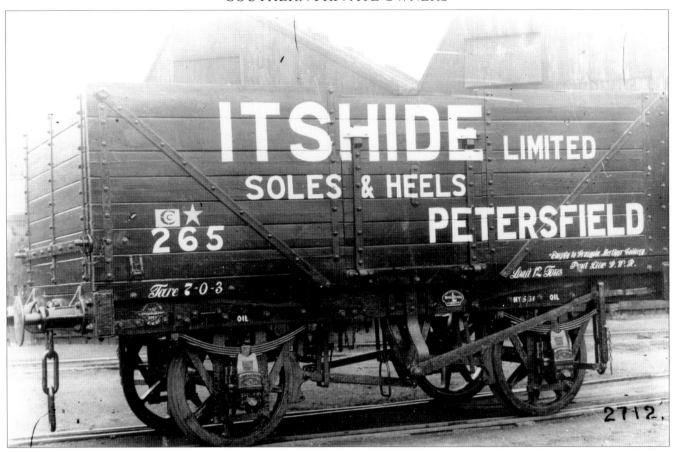

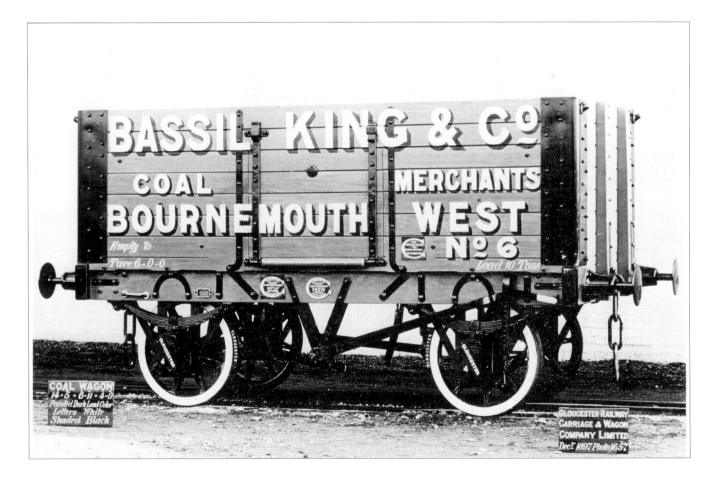

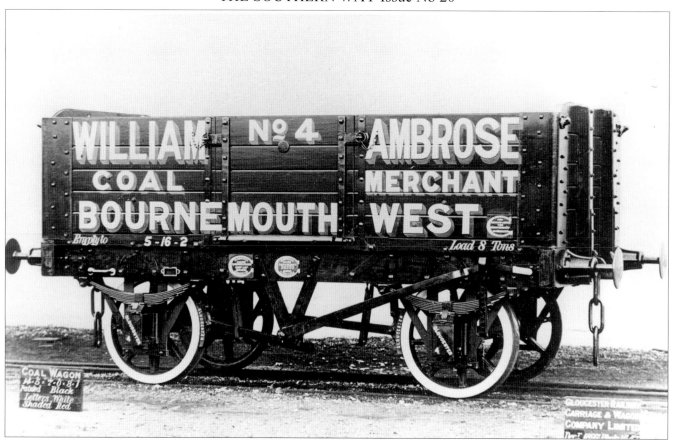

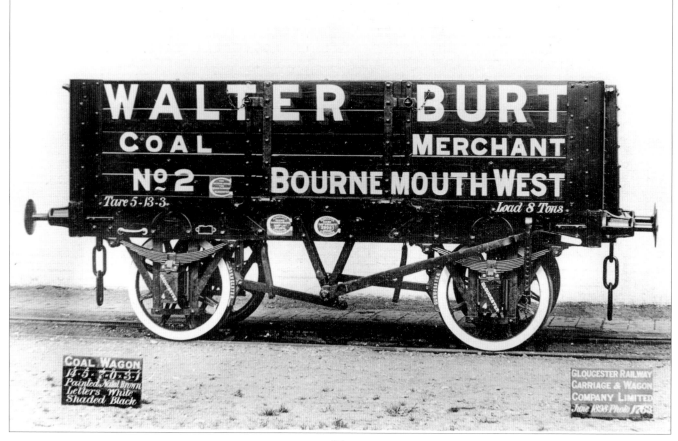

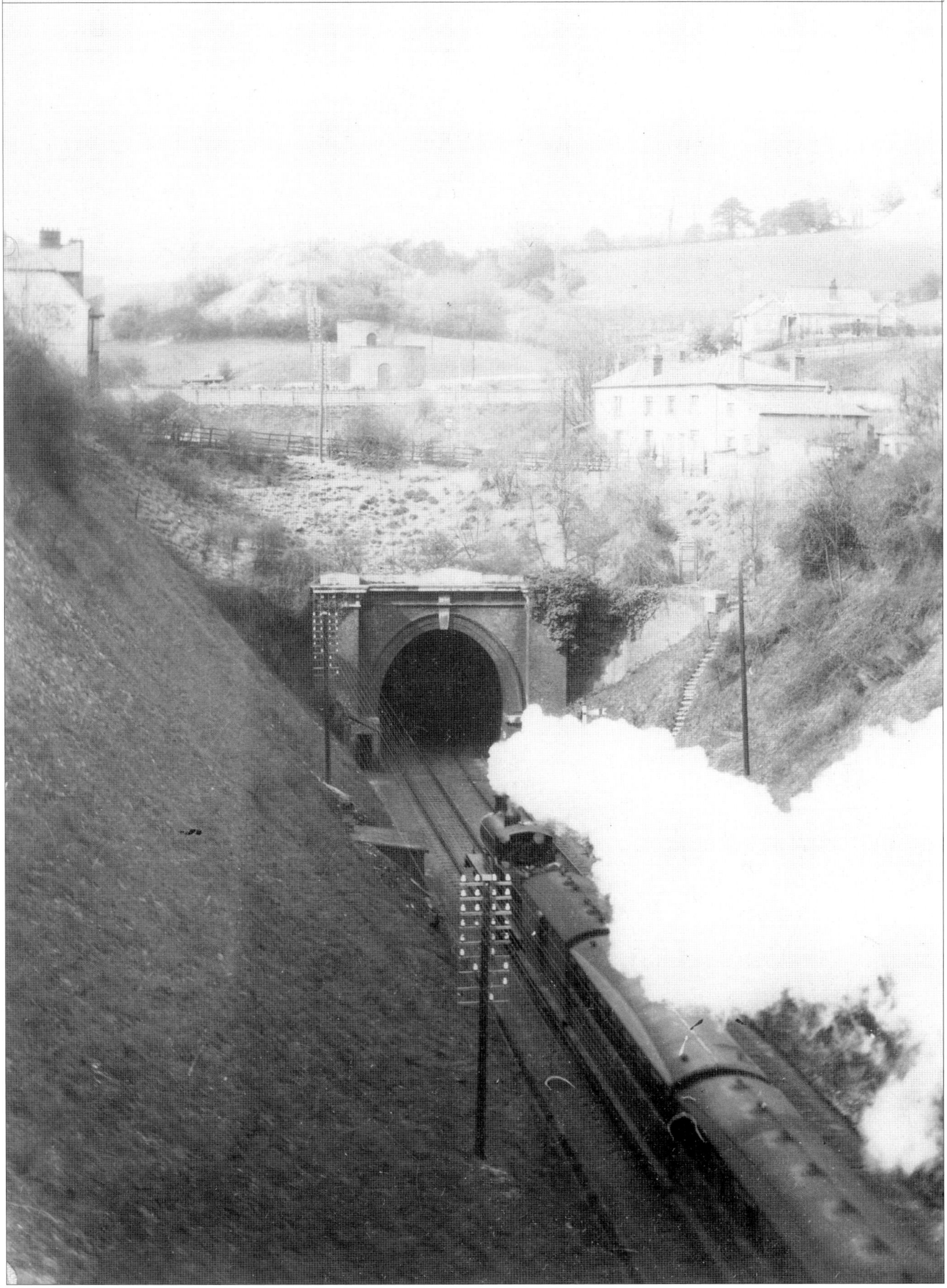

Above - Bill's first signal box, Hampton Court Junction where he was a booking lad from April 1947 until September 1949. The view was taken from a passing train in 1960 by which time comments, 'There were now tie-bards holding things together'. Dating from June 1936, the box contained a 45 lever 'A2' frame, it was closed from 1 March 1970.

Left - Bill admits he might not have started under the auspices of the Southern Railway but at least his letter inviting him to apply to work on the railway was produced on proper SR stationary!

SOUTHERN RAILWAY
───────
STATION MASTER'S OFFICE,
SURBITON.
8th April   48

Telephone:
ELMBRIDGE 1844.

My
Your

Reference.

Mr W.Trigg.
80 Cleveland Road.
Surbiton.

Dear Sir,

    With reference to your call at my office, A vanancy exists at Hampton Court Junction Signal Box for a Booking Boy, the duties consist of recording the times of the trains as they pass the Box.

    If this appeals to you perhaps you will call and see me.

                    Yours faithfully,

                    B F Johnson

                    Stationmaster.

FROM SCHOOLBOY TO SIGNAL BOX
THE MEMORIES OF BILL TRIGG
Part 2
(Continued from Issue No 18)

The winter of 1947/48 was very bad, with heavy falls of snow that lay about for weeks. It disrupted all forms of transport, burst water pipes and power cuts were the order of the day and food rationing was still in force from the war years.

I seized on this opportunity to suggest that it might be time to explore the possibility of employment on the railway. My father gave the matter some thought, and said he would have a word with the Station Master at Surbiton to see if there were any vacancies in the uniform grades. He did as promised and told me to write my application to the SM which got the reply shown. An interview followed, after which I was told I was accepted, assuming I passed the Medical. This was at London Bridge - I passed.

I cannot therefore claim to have been a true 'Southern' railwayman for I started after nationalisation, on the 19 April 1948. Even so it was still run almost exactly as per Southern methods, something that would continue for many years to come.

My first role was as booking boy at Hampton Court Junction: the signalman on duty was Bert Merritt with booking boy Arthur Alden, they both made me welcome, I remember it was a very strange experience; it seemed there were bells and buzzers going all the time with the levers being thrown back and forth. There were also telephones ringing and being answered (there were six plus a small switch-board).

After four weeks I must admit I still found the whole system of working very complex. When asked their opinion of me by the local station master, two of the three signalmen said I was not up to their expected standard: however Bert Merritt said he would take me on, provided the boys and the men rotated together. The original arrangement being that the boys had rotated the opposite way round to the signalmen. This suggestion was agreed to, thus signalman Bert Merritt and I became one pair of the three covering the twenty-four hours around the standard three-shift arrangement.

Bert himself came from a long line of signalmen although, as a youth and out of respect for my elders, I never dared ask too much, something I have regretted in later years. What I did glean was that Bert 'senior' had been employed in the old Waterloo 'A' box, which must have been quite a job. He also had an elder brother who worked as a signalman at Waterloo. When I started on the job Bert's brother would phone and say "The 1.25am West of England paper train is just leaving". Bert would respond by stating he would deal with it in due course and that his brother should go back to his shunting movements! He would continue that they (at Waterloo) would be lost if they had to deal with trains running at express speeds: all good-hearted banter taken in a good spirit.

On other occasions I would answer the phone and say I would pass the message on, but his brother would insist on speaking to Bert. Now the response from Bert was that his brother was worried in case he was resting, especially during the quieter periods of the night shift.

It was Bert who patiently finished teaching me the duties of a booking boy: recording each train that passed the signal box, and reporting to control the passing times of all freight and any special traffic including paper trains (there were five each night). In addition we had to report the passing times of troop and boat trains, all to the control office at Woking.

Hampton Court Junction was the last signal box included in the program of colour light signalling from Waterloo to Hampton Court Junction in 1937. The box was equipped with a forty-five lever Westinghouse frame with an illuminated diagram, with Sykes Lock and Block to Esher, Hampton Court and the Guildford New Line.

The signal box at Surbiton was the first of what was to become known as the greenhouse type, but Hampton Court Junction, although built at the same time, was to an earlier design. A new box was provided as the original cabin had been of all wood construction and not suitable for the new colour light electrical equipment. Unfortunately there had been no allowance in the cost of the re-signalling for a new signal box at HCJ, hence one had to be provided quickly and also as cheaply as possible. Another explanation why we did not get a smart modern structure was that at Surbiton the signal box was within sight of the then new station built in ferro-concrete to the design of Mr. J.R. Scott. (This is now a grade two listed building: for some years the tower clock told lies, but even that is now honest!) It is a pity that at Surbiton the 1930s signal box was demolished very quickly in the 1970s, for the simple reason it was holding up development of a car park for a new supermarket nearby.

This page and opposite - Subiton opened on 28 June 1936 the one box replacing the former East and West cabins. Inside was a 52 lever Westinghouse 'A2' frame. From the interior illustration it can be seen that train describers were in use together with full track circuiting and associated illuminated diagram. The short handle levers indicated electrically operated equipment. The exterior view dates from c1938.

. At Hampton Court Junction there were three-aspect colour light signals on the down local and through lines. The down Hampton Court home signal was a semaphore as was the Cobham line and down local and through starting signals. On the up lines, the local and through line home signals were three aspect colour light, while for Esher East semaphore signals were provided with approach colour lights below them.

The up Cobham and Hampton Court home signals were similar semaphores with approach lights below. Interestingly, at that time, the up Hampton Court line was provided with an inner and outer up distant, numbers 33 & 34 in the frame, and these were located on Thames Ditton's up home and starting signals. I am not certain but assume this dates back to steam, when on race days at Hurst Park it would assist return trains up the incline to the junction.

I was lucky to have been on duty when the 1948 locomotive exchanges took place. Work in the box kept me busy and the only lasting memory I have was on the day the LNER A4 'Seagull' went down with the 12.00 noon, 'Devon Belle', but had the misfortune to fail near Salisbury with a hot axle box on the tender. Bert and I were on late turn and when eventually the A4 limped by slowly running light engine on the up local line making for Nine Elms Loco, Bert was somewhat caustic with his comments,

suggesting none too politely that the crew took it home without delay. A Southern man through and through was Bert!

There was a service booked up the local from Esher just after 4.00 pm weekdays that originated from Eastleigh at 1.15 pm bound for the loop at Clapham Junction. This was made up of various items of coaching stock that had undergone repair and normally was hauled by a member of the T14 Class. The practice was for this train to be brought to a stand at the up local home signal to await a pathway on the through line behind the Atlantic Coast Express. Officially the working timetable referred to this train as the 10.17am Ilfracombe, although Bert insisted it be recorded as the 9.52am Padstow, that being the furthest point of the Atlantic Coast Express.

When we were able to give the T14 the road, we would stand at the window ready to admire the effort put into getting the train moving with red hot coals coming out the chimney like a Roman candle, so much so that Bert referred to it as a Brocks Fireworks Special! The driver would be making a series of hand signals which we did not quite understand, but had a very good idea what he was trying to convey. I felt sorry for the fireman, it must have been disheartening, for as fast as he put coal in the firebox, it was out of the chimney.

Some of Bert's advice I still remember. One was that if you are not happy to work weekends, evenings and bank holidays, including Christmas Day (we ran a train service on Christmas Day in those days), you would be better off looking for employment in some other industry. Another was that as we worked in the signal box for eight hours of each day, twenty days out of twenty-one, we were spending almost a third of our life there, so the place should be kept clean and tidy - like home. One more was, that once a decision had been made, stick with it: to change your mind could cause confusion, or at worst disaster. (This last phrase of Bert's should be interpreted as 'once a route or signal has been set, do not change it unless absolutely vital. The driver might have glanced at the indication once already'.)

Perhaps the most important was that if you managed to lock the frame up so that the lever you wanted to operate would not release, place all the levers back in the frame and start again. Never use the Sykes release key, it was better to toss it out of the window and stop and think. If after all this you still decided you must use it, go and find it. The idea being that it gave time to consider, instead of the ramifications of making a hasty decision. Having read 'Red for Danger' a fair number of accidents contained therein might have been avoided if Bert's advice had been followed.

Like most other booking boys both at HCJ and elsewhere, we were encouraged to operate the frame and instruments - under the watchful eye of the signalman of course. On the lighter side, Bert had a shove half-penny

board and was a keen player. This came into regular use to pass the time on nights. Nearby another signalman and his booking boy were avid Ludo players, whilst others would spend hours chatting on the 'bus'(omnibus telephone circuit to which many could listen) extolling the virtues of gardening, bell ringing, politics, running the railway – of course – as well as numerous other subjects.

One funny little story related to me by Arthur Alden, the booking boy who was my relief, was that one day he had arrived on duty at six o'clock but Bill Barwick his signalman had not arrived to relieve Bert. Bert could not of course leave the box unattended so after waiting awhile asked Arthur to cycle round to where Bill lodged to establish if he was sick, or if he had just overslept. Arthur told me that on arrival at Bill's lodgings he knocked on the door and was greeted by Bill's landlady calling out "What do you want?" Arthur opened the letter box and called "Bert wants to know if Bill is coming to work today?" This was greeted with silence so and after a while Arthur knocked again asking the same question. Again there was the "What do you want?" reply. This continued for some time, until Bill suddenly burst forth still in the process of getting dressed. He had simply overslept, so took over duty somewhat late. Arthur it appeared had been having a conversation with the landlady's mynah bird!

Speaking of Bill he was a bit of an oddity. In those early days of British Railways we were still being issued with Southern Railway uniform complete with

SR. buttons. But as each issue was made Bill would set to work and remove the SR buttons and replace them with his own set of L&SWR ones, all very highly polished.

Bill also had a very useful piece of equipment in his locker, it was a ex-WD first world war 'Signals' telescope, about two foot long when closed down. It was used to look at train head codes for if, as sometimes happened, Surbiton forgot to describe a down train, with this you could see if it was an "H Bar" bound for Guildford via Cobham, and the New Line. More importantly there was an early warning of the area Inspector walking down the track, on one of his surprise visits or any other strangers coming our way.

Another of Bill's oddities was that for whatever reason he did not bother to collect his wages on a regular basis, something very unusual for a railwayman. It culminated in him being advised by the station master that he would be forced to take action by paying these moneys in as unpaid wages.

One strange happening was on a train on its way down from Surbiton which approached blowing its whistle. As it passed a knob of coal was thrown out with a piece of paper wrapped around it. We were asked to inform Woking station that a replacement firing shovel was needed - the fireman had lost his in the firebox. I assume they made it to Woking and a replacement was indeed obtained.

Summer Saturdays were always busy. The early turn would start with light engines down from Nine Elms or Clapham Yard to the carriage sidings at Esher or Walton-on-Thames ready to pick up the empty stock. Usually these were M7 tanks and would struggle back with a train that might consist of twelve or even thirteen empty bogies, bound for Waterloo.

These trains of empty stock would mingle with the Saturday business trains to Waterloo (Saturday morning was then part of the working week). In the down direction the bulk of the traffic before noon was from Waterloo to the coast with destinations ranging from Portsmouth for the Isle of Wight, Bournemouth, Swanage, Weymouth and Ilfracombe and Padstow in the west. This holiday traffic flow would ease around mid-day, only to be replaced by the homeward business trains after the half-day at work. After this we would see a succession of troop leave specials heading for Waterloo, usually occupied by those on thirty-six hour passes, whilst starting part way through this were the first of the returning holiday makers. Fortunately on a Saturday all the steam workings carried duty numbers on the smokebox which was a great help to us booking lads in identifying the working against the timetable and special traffic notices.

On one occasion I remember an M7 on a rake of empties from bound for Waterloo, running bunker first and working quite hard having being diverted off the local to the through line - the middle of the crossover being immediately under the fly-over bridge that carries the down Hampton Court line. As the engine passed under the bridge the crew suffered a blow-back through the firebox that filled the cab with flames. I suspect they been anticipating this for they were both very quickly out on the running plate on either side. Fortunately as the engine cleared the flyover the fire went back in the firebox and the crew went back inside the cab, giving us a wave as they passed.

Saturdays ended with a procession of light engines bound for Nine Elms, that had left Waterloo and travelled on a circular route via Staines and Chertsey with empty stock to reach Oatlands sidings and the Race Platforms at Esher ready to berth the empty stock ready for the next Saturday when there would be a repeat performance.

One of the less pleasant jobs for us boys each week was to empty the Elsan toilet bucket when on the early turn week, Friday being the appointed day. We would take this down the two flights of stairs with great care. Next the booking boy would dig a hole near the signal box deep enough to hold the contents and carefully cover it over. It's amazing to think we were doing this only thirteen miles from Waterloo. You just had to take note where your colleague had been digging the previous week!

Left - Coal empties at Surbiton.

Opposite *- The third rail and snow never worked well together. Fortunately scenes such as this were rare - Surbiton again but this time mantled by snow.*

My colleague as booking boy, Arthur, was a bit older than me, so he was conscripted for National Service into the Royal Engineers a few months earlier than would happen to me.

When this happened, we two boys that were left had to revert to either early or late turn working, so rotating with the three signalmen. Fortunately under Bert's guidance I had now mastered the role; it had just taken me a bit longer. One of the other men I now worked with was Bill Trayhorne, a dapper little man who had a brother who was a professional opera singer. I suspect Bill felt he was just as capable for he would burst forth into song at the least provocation.

He and I were late turn one summer Saturday. As each service passed we crossed off the up trains on the list of numbers that corresponded with the engine head boards. It had got to the point where the next working on the through line should be a troop leave train from Tidworth, booked to run on the up local line ready for a stop at Surbiton. This would allow the 4.34 pm 'Bournemouth Belle' to pass by at 6.31pm. Consequently Bill had the road ready for a crossing from the main to the local line. We then received the "Is line clear?" bell signal. Bill responded. The route was set and the signal cleared. Next came 'Train entering section" from Esher, whilst soon after our first view under the viaduct bridge was of a locomotive carrying not the West of England headcode as expected but a Bournemouth line code. Yes it was the Bournemouth Belle, the crew making some very queer gesticulations on the footplate at us. Bill was on the box to box phone to Surbiton in a flash, I expect the crew were even more confused when Surbiton turned them out on the through line again. The Tidworth did eventually turn up running very late, on the up the local line

There was a signal lamp-man who attended our semaphore signals. I knew him as 'Sagger' Knight, who would arrive along the cess on his bicycle. He was armed with two cans full of paraffin, one each hung on the handlebars and an ex-army pack on his back. Once his job was done he would call in for a cup of tea and then set off back again.

I remember being asked by Bill Trayhorn to go down the track to Esher West box on an errand. Jack Cudlip, a relief signalman on duty there, lived at Worplesdon, and had an apple orchard in his garden. He had brought a sandbag full of apples up for Bill. I went with a will, this being my first opportunity to walk the line to Esher. It was a lovely sunny afternoon (funny how memory always recalls the nice days). I remember looking at the impressive semaphore gantries for the up starting and home signals and even managed to get a look in through the locked door of Esher East signal box and the ground frame cabin at London end of the centre platform. This controlled entry to the goods yard with release from Esher West. Both the East and West boxes at Esher were of all-wood construction, dating from LSWR days. One nice touch in the West box was the provision of an old fashioned wooden settle seat, that extended from the floor to about eight feet high, this had a normal position against the back wall, but was hinged to allow it to be brought out at right angles to the wall to give some protection from the weather that would otherwise come in through the door in winter: I never came across anything like this in any other box I went in. The West box was provided with the renowned race platform starting signal that slotted into its post when not in use. Also provided was control of the down line Mole Intermediate signals which had replaced Mole signal box sometime in the past.

To be continued.

DEEPDENE HOUSE
Images and notes by Roger Sawyer

Scenes of the wartime HQ of the Southern Railway at Deepdene House near Dorking. (See also P81 S/W Special No 5 - Wartime Southern part 2.)

Above - Taken from the lawn, the ground and first floor were occupied by the Chief Accountant's Department and the top floor by the CCE Bridge Office.

Left - Again from the lawn showing the wartime extension which when taken housed the Treasurer and his offices.

Above - The front of the building with the car park and bus turning area. Also at the front of the building was a putting green, during WW2 this had been where a number of radio masts stood. Nearby and driven into the ground horizontally, were three tube-size train tunnels, these houses the 'hardened' offices for operational control staff and where the railway telephone exchange was located. The last named remained operational until the building closed in the late 1960s. The grounds themselves were well kept and included a tulip tree. The residential gardening staff not permitted to touch this without staff from Kew Gardens being present. *Below -* The stable block then known as the Annexe which housed the SR Savings Bank and Superannuation Fund offices.

Top - Farningham Road station from Homesfield Farm bridge looking east circa 1950, photographer unknown.
Bottom - An unusual, from the formation, down coastal express passes Farningham Road in April 1959. Donald Knowler

FARNINGHAM ROAD

A STATION IN KENT

John Woodhead

A brief history

As in many rural communities across the country, the impact of the coming of the railway to South Darenth, Horton Kirby and Sutton-at-Hone in the mid-nineteenth century was to be both significant and permanent. Prior to the opening of the station, the outside world was accessible only by poorly maintained roads. The railway immediately brought markets closer to manufacturers and farmers alike and, in this area, led to the expansion of the paper mill. As a consequence, the number of workers required to meet increased production resulted in South Darenth being transformed from a rural hamlet to a village with an industrial complexion.

The East Kent Railway began life in 1853, opening the Faversham to Chatham section on 25 January 1858 and extending it from Chatham to Rochester Bridge two months later. In August 1859 the East Kent Railway became the London, Chatham & Dover Railway and 'Farningham' station opened to passengers on 3 December 3 1860: the same time as St. Mary Cray, Strood and the rest of the new line from Rochester Bridge to Bickley.

Put simply, the line came about as a result of a battle between the London, Chatham & Dover Railway and the already established South Eastern Railway in a race to win the custom of passengers travelling to the continent. By the mid-1840s the SER had already listed numerous proposals for lines to the coast, opening lines to Folkestone and then Dover by 1844. However, they appear not to have taken seriously the challenge from the emerging competition. O.S. Nock records that: "At the end of 1849 the question of constructing a direct line of railway from

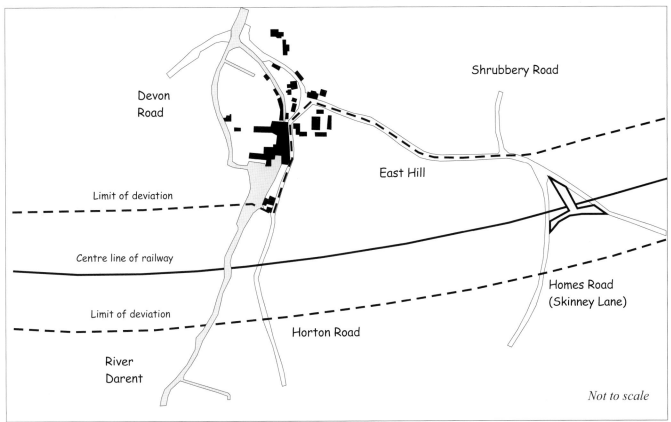

Drawn from the deposited plans of the East Kent Railway (Western Extension) 1858. Of particular interest are the details of the buildings in South Darenth, the various branches of the river, and the original road layout to the east. The proposed realignment of the roads, forming what is now the Homes bridge, has a darker outline.

A general view of the station in April 1953, showing the uncovered, lattice-work footbridge. The shadow of the water tower and hose can be seen on the foot crossing in the foreground.

R. C Riley /Transport Treasury

Strood to Dover was actively discussed, and on 29 January 1850, a large meeting was held in Rochester. It was pointed out during this meeting how great the saving in distance and time would be between the towns in East Kent and London by the construction of such a line. Faversham, it was stated, stood to gain most, to the extent of 34 miles and even Dover – primarily the goal of the SER – the saving in distance would be 16 miles".

After application to parliament, a western extension from Chatham to St Mary Cray was granted to the London, Chatham & Dover Railway in 1858. The first London, Chatham & Dover Railway train ran from

Rochester to Bickley on 12 October 1860 and began a regular service to Victoria over lines belonging to other companies two months later. R.W. Kidner states that, a few months later, there were: "Five trains daily, and one each from Chatham and Faversham only. One of the best trains, the 5 pm down did the trip to Canterbury in 2 hours and 10 minutes, stopping at Crystal Palace, Beckenham, St Mary Cray, Farningham Road, Chatham, Sittingbourne

Tom Ludlow, who was born in South Darenth, spent his working life with British Rail, a major part of his personal involvement being to seek out historical records to establish the company's legal obligations and negotiate with

Looking towards Swanley from the up platform in 1960, with a clear view of the engine shed and the water crane.

D. K. Jones Collection

An early postcard of the station showing the covered footbridge. The photographer, Ferdinand Kehrhahn, was a German émigré who started taking pictures of South Darenth circa 1906. To avoid internment in the first World War he embarked for New York from Liverpool but was detained by the captain and returned to England.

FARNINGHAM RD. STATION, SOUTH DARENTH.

its neighbours. In his words: "The procedure for obtaining parliamentary authority for railway schemes is to publish plans and consult with local and County authorities as well as all landowners and tenants affected by the proposals. These plans with all other documentation are laid before parliament for approval. Essentially the plans must show the line of the proposed railway also the 'limits of deviation' showing the extent of the lands that can be acquired for such purposes; the property to be affected or purchased to be described in a book of reference relating to the plans, with the names of reputed owners. The centre plans must also show gradients and cross sections where appropriate and the documents are now identified as *Deposited Plans and Books of reference for The East Kent Railway Act (Western Extension) 1858.*"

From these documents we can identify the most significant landowners at the time as being the Muggeridge family, although Edward Cresy and the 'Provost and Fellowes of Queens College Oxford' are also named. The properties required by the railway company through the villages were predominantly meadow and arable land, although also identified within the limits of deviation were garden sheds, the mill pond and the farm at the bottom of East Hill opposite the 'Jolly Millers'. The 1858 plans show the limits of deviation stayed constant and parallel to the south of the proposed line, but to the north the limit ran down the centre of East Hill, along Horton Road towards where the viaduct was eventually constructed and then skirted the Mill and the Mill owners' house before returning to run parallel with the centre line of the planned railway again.

Tom Ludlow theorizes on the railway company's decision to buy an unusually large amount of land to the east of South Darenth, prior to the line's construction: 'From the

viaduct heading east the embankment continued over farmland, but here it seems that the railway company was authorised to take much more land, the 'deviation' limit extended up East Hill to a point where the Homes Bridge is now. There were no buildings between East Hill and the railway line and I would guess that either the landowners at the time did not want to sell part of their land, so made the railway buy it all, or, the railway company acquired it all as a working site for the considerable earthworks in the village. The top part of New Road was handed over to the local authority as late as the 1940s, which rather suggests that the railway did purchase these lands for some reason, then sold them off as they became redundant".

The bridge over the railway, known locally as Homes Bridge, was built to carry both Homes Road, (Skinney Lane) and Rabbits Road. These were two different roads joined together, then taken over the railway by one bridge, and became one road, now East Hill. This was before New Road existed.

The engineering and construction demands required to span The Darent Valley were considerable. The viaduct, the embankments, (to the west), and the deep cuttings, (to the east), needed to carry the line across the Darent, (thus limiting gradients but creating the 'Farningham Dip'), are estimated to have taken approximately two years. Construction work therefore began only a year or so after Edward Cresy had written his 'Tour Round the Parish of Horton Kirby'. The floor of the Darent Valley at this crossing point would have consisted of water-meadows, pasture and watercress beds and as well as diverting the Darent through the viaduct, engineers also had to create a culvert to house a secondary or overflow channel. They also had to construct the brick bridge over the Farningham – Dartford road. Some three million bricks

A Dover to Victoria service in May 1938. Note the covered wagons in the signal box sidings.

H. C. Casserley

were required to complete the ten-arched viaduct and it is difficult to imagine the reaction of the people living locally as they watched the structure and associated embankments rise from the valley. The viaduct, at 120 feet high, was completed in June 1860, designed by Sir William Cubitt and built using London Yellow Stock , (supplied by the Aylesford Pottery Company), the same brick as was used for the construction of the station buildings. The embankments are likely to have been constructed from the spoil removed from tunnels and cuttings elsewhere on the line, as well as, it is suggested, from the chalk quarry to the west of the station which eventually became the goods yard.

Construction of the line would likely have been by itinerant workers, navvies who followed opportunities for railway construction employment around the country, living in temporary accommodation where they could find it, and even, it is suggested, living rough in Farningham or Rams Woods. Predominantly Irish, escaping the harsh economic conditions at home, they were the lifeblood of this country's railway expansionism in the mid-Nineteenth Century, providing cheap labour long before wide scale and effective mechanisation. The terrace of bungalows at Wood Street, Swanley village, was built by the railway company to house workers digging the cuttings and constructing the line from Farningham Road to Swanley. Work and conditions were clearly dangerous and hard and there were a number of accidents, including a report of a fatality at Longfield Hill in May 1859.

There is speculation as to why the station was sited so far from Farningham itself, at the time an important stopping point on the journey from London to Dover. Local landowners' and farmers' attitudes to the coming of railways in other parts of the country were, at the time, very wary, with fears that livestock would abort and that the new means of steam-driven travel would be dangerous and thus unpopular so close to a large community.

The main station buildings were almost identical to those built contemporaneously at Sole Street. The latter had a Post Office, something that never reached Farningham Road, although it did have, and still retains, its post box. In 1895, when Henry Thomas Hards was station master, the post box was clearly of great local importance, being cleared three times a day. George Parker is recorded at this time as being not only the coal merchant but also agent to 'Shepherd, Neame and Co. brewers and the London Manure Co.' This is explored in more detail later. In 1922 Sydney Charles Hannam is recorded as station master and Farningham Road had by now a telegraph office.

John Minnis in *Southern Country Stations'* describes the character of the buildings erected in 1859: "With the advance towards London in 1860 another design of country station appeared, no less austere and plain than those of two years previously. Stations to this design were erected at St. Mary Cray, Farningham Road and Sole Street. The principal difference between them and the earlier type was that instead of being two storeyed throughout they comprised a single storey booking office attached to a two storey residence which did not have a gable facing the track. The dour appearance was not noticeably improved by painting the brickwork. All survive with the exception of St. Mary Cray which was rebuilt in the 1930s".

The station also differs from other LC&DR stations of the period in that it was built without a canopy or porch by the booking office door.

David Glasspool from Kent Rail, describes the station as: "Typical London Chatham and Dover Railway intermediate station architecture, constructed from the now familiar light-coloured brick of the company. The main station building here was situated on the up side, two storeys high, backing onto a steep approach way and incorporating the usual accommodation seen along the line for the Station Master. The building was flanked on its western side by another typical LC&DR structure – the single-track brick-built goods shed – and on its eastern elevation by a single-storey pitched roof storage building. The unusual bricked enclosure (next to the Station Master's house to the east on the down side), is thought to be the former toilets, typical of the period (such open air facilities are still in use at Gravesend Central)".

It is worth noting, however, that Tony Carter, a former Station Master who lived in the house, regards this last suggestion as being highly unlikely.

David Glasspool continues: "The down side was somewhat unusual by lacking any form of passenger accommodation, but a very imposing feature was situated on this platform: a two-storey high water tower. It is strange as to why such a structure would have been located at this initially insignificant station, which does suggest that it came into use concurrent with the Gravesend West branch in 1886 – most trains on this line began and terminated at Farningham". He continues with more detail of the original goods shed: "This was a through building and was served by a wagon turntable at its western end – a reversal manoeuvre into the shed provided access to a lengthy siding, positioned where the Corus complex is now. There were also three more sidings which needed to be accounted for: two of these were again located on the up side, but to the east of the station building. The final siding lay on the down side, at the London end of the platform and trailed off in the westward direction. Sandwiched in-between this siding and the platform end was a signal box of Saxby and Farmer design, which most likely appeared in 1886 with the Gravesend West branch and an additional siding, the latter laid parallel with the existing track. From the outset a track crossing was in use at the London ends of the platforms, but later this was superseded by a covered footbridge. Most such structures came into existence on both LC&DR and SER railway networks during the 1890s, when the Board of Trade began tightening standards and finance was available for such structures. Finally, at the turn of the century, a single track connection with an adjacent chalk pit was installed, this being situated adjacent to the station's goods yard on the up side. This was coupled with the addition of a further siding on the down side by the signal box *(circa 1876)*, and the revision of the approach tracks to the goods shed.

Since that time there have been other changes and alterations, some greater than others. The water tower lost its tank in response to the Southern Railway's 1939 suburban electrification of the 'Chatham' line as far as Gillingham, Electric Multiple Units commencing scheduled passenger operation on 2 July that year. All was not lost for this imposing structure however, as its large brick base was reused in the new role of a waiting room – it must certainly have been the largest intermediate station waiting facility along the route! Push-pull operation on the Gravesend West branch had been a feature for many years and when this line became single track in 1959, Farningham Road became the token exchange point.

15 June 1959 marked the complete cessation of regular steam haulage on the 'Chatham' main line, with the completion of the Kent Coast Electrification Scheme's 'Phase 1', but Farningham Road retained an operational goods shed for nearly nine years more, closure coming in May 1968. During the 1970s the former water tank base succumbed and the footbridge lost its roof, but sidings were retained on both the up and down sides, to the west of the platforms *(photographic evidence from elsewhere suggests that the footbridge lost its roof earlier, circa 1954)*. Those on the down side were used for rolling stock storage, but the single siding still extant on the up side was utilised by British Steel until 1980. Closure of the signal box followed on 12 June 1983 when control was passed to the Victoria panel.

In the summer of 2003, during track repair and maintenance: 'a track crane vehicle collided with the lattice footbridge, damaging it to a state deemed beyond economical repair. For the best part of a year, the station made do with a temporary basic wood and scaffolding structure. However, even before this was finally erected, the only way passengers could cross between the two platforms – legitimately – was the circuitous route of the footpath on the down side, the main road, then up the steep incline of the station approach, (or the reverse of this). To prevent passengers from taking a shortcut over the tracks at the west end of the platforms, physical blockades were installed on the ramps!

Another piece of equipment worth mentioning was the water crane used to fill locomotives' tanks. It was situated just to the west of the up platform, although a map of 1885 shows a second water crane at the end of the coast-bound platform. In 1909 there was also a 5-ton capacity goods shed crane in the goods yard.

As well as being a centre for the delivery and receiving of goods traffic, Farningham Road was also host to special excursions, run by a number of diverse groups. An extract from the Horton Parish Magazine of July 1899 describes a church outing to the seaside: "The Choir and

their friends assembled on the platform at Farningham Road Station to the number of forty odd, and went to Margate by the excursion train, which was stopped for them at about eight o'clock. At twenty past eight at Margate Station, the whole party was brought safely home; the Railway Company in a larking mood, taking us up to Bromley and then sending us back to our own station by a slow train, and (wonderful to relate) charging us nothing extra for the additional twenty miles."

The following month saw a Young Men and Boys' Bible Class excursion: "The early morning of the 8 August saw a party of 137 people gathered on the platform of Farningham Road Station, and by the 7.08 train the start for Hastings was made via Swanley, Otford and Sevenoaks, and the destination was reached in safety – in comfort also, thanks to reserved carriages."

The day over, they arrived at Hastings Station for the journey home: "Again were our carriages reserved for us, and we much appreciated the comfort of this, but many of us felt far from pleased when some of the lamps went out, leaving us in total darkness, while others had to watch the gradual dropping of the oil with the fear that it might splash against the flame. Owing to these little catastrophes we can hardly say the journey was devoid of excitement; still, even then, though the train crawled along, everyone was cheerful and ready to make the best of things. It should also be mentioned that at Otford suddenly it was discovered somebody was missing. However, it transpired that he had gone by a fast train to Bromley and on to Farningham Road."

The station has undergone a number of name changes, particularly in its infancy. On 1st April 1861 it became 'Farningham & Sutton' but reverted to simply 'Farningham' four months later. In September 1869 it was renamed 'Farningham Road' but changed again to 'Farningham Road & Sutton-at-Hone' 16 months later in January 1872. Maps and timetables have subsequently referred to the station as 'Farningham Road', a name it has used since 1970.

Platform signs have also advertised itself as the 'Station for Homes for Little Boys'. The Homes itself was served for some years from 8 July 1870 by its own platform. The boys would travel down from north London alighting on a down-side platform next to the bridge at the top of East Hill and then climb the steep steps cut into the embankment in order to reach their new home. This platform was capable of holding eight large carriages and was also used on special occasions by benefactors and wealthy visitors, although it clearly was not in existence in July 1866, as an account of the laying of the foundation stone in that year records. A special train from London took invited guests to Farningham station which was, "...most tastefully decorated with flowers and evergreen; for this we are indebted to the skill and energy of Mr Robert Palmer, our indefatigable station master". The viaduct was also decorated with evergreen, flags and festoons. An account of the summer fete exactly ten years later however, recorded that, "...as usual on the day of the summer fete the Home was gay with bunting, and, on arrival of the special train from London at the platform adjoining the gates, there was a large influx of ladies and gentlemen." Open days were held every year with as many as 2,000 visitors arriving by special trains from London. The first note of the platform's use was on 11 October 1870 when one JS Martin requested that the gates at the top of the steps be left open to allow access from the platform.

In *'The History of a Great Charity – The Home For Little Boys'*, probably written sometime in the 1960s, H.O.Tester reported that: "The Home in those early days even had its own arrival platform for the benefit of groups of visitors arriving from London. Travel by rail was the only practical method in those days and for convenience the London, Chatham and Dover Railway provided a platform just outside the main gate of the Home. A path was cut from the platform to the road, and over the railway bridge, to the Homes. The platform fell into disuse some 50 years ago but traces of its existence can still be seen. The exclusive arrival platform was appreciated by the many who travelled by train to attend the annual Festival. Concessionary rates were agreed and the Railway Company provided for parties of not less than 4 persons to travel the double journey first class at a single fare."

An account in the same magazine two years later in 1901, on the subject of excursions, reads: "But surely none can have been pleasanter than that of the employees of the Horton Kirby Paper Works, their families, and the Bible Class lads, to Margate and Ramsgate on July 8. Brilliant sunshine, (which lasted all day too!), Pleasant greetings at Farningham Station, (does Mr Hale know everybody, we wonder). A quick journey down, with no stopping – think of it, you who travel by the 6.38 – our destination reached before 8.30".

In 1905 the magazine reported on the Young Women's Bible Class outing to Folkestone: "August 30 - 6.40 am – Farningham Road. Every assistance was rendered to our party by the officials on the railway". The Church Choir had a similar experience, travelling down to Margate for the day in July 1906: "The early start at about 6.30 am was made without any weary waiting and owing, to the courtesy of the railway officials, without any uncomfortable crowding."

In 1902 the station came to the attention of the national press when 'The Times' reported a near catastrophic accident, averted only by the actions of the signalman.

RAILWAY SMASH AT FARNINGHAM VIADUCT,
GOODS TRAIN DIVIDES AND COLLIDES,
EXPRESS'S NARROW ESCAPE

Parker's sidings are on the right as the 2.27 service leaves for Gravesend in May 1938. H. C. Casserley

"A disaster was narrowly averted early on Thursday morning at Farningham viaduct, where the main line to Chatham passes over the Darenth Valley at a height of about 111ft, The midnight express from London to Chatham had left Swanley, and was nearing the viaduct, when a goods train traversing it was suddenly wrecked by the rear portion becoming detached and colliding with the fore part. Both rails were blocked with a mass of wreckage, and trucks were thrown down the viaduct. Those in charge fortunately escaped, and made an effort to communicate with the signalman at Farningham–road station to save the express. This was not possible, but the signalman, named Bailey, had heard a crash from the viaduct, and though he could not tell what had happened, he decided to turn the signals against the express, and save it rushing upon destruction. The train was brought back to London and re-despatched by the way of the North Kent line."

A second account read as follows: "Another railway accident of almost precisely the same character as that which occurred a few weeks since, happened just outside Farningham-road station on the London, Chatham and Dover Railway, early on Thursday morning. About one o'clock a goods train was proceeding from Fawkham towards Farningham-road, when one of the couplings broke. The driver was not aware of this until he slowed up to stop at the latter station, when, after the forepart of the train had just crossed the viaduct, the hind trucks, which were following on down the slight incline, collided with the other part of the train. About a dozen trucks were derailed, and fouled the line, but the traffic being turned on to the down line, very little delay was caused. Several of the trucks rolled down the embankment, while a pair of wheels of one of the trucks gathered such pace in descending the bank that they crossed the road leading from the station to Horton Kirby and finally stopped several yards out in the meadow. Fortunately there was no personal injury. The sight of the embankment being strewn with champagne bottles, brought the particulars of the previous accident well to mind, but on this occasion the owners had the satisfaction of consuming the contents for the trucks contained quality goods."

The Homes for Little Boys Old Boys' Journal provided more information about the heroic signalman: "Bailey has served the Chatham Railway for thirty-six years, and for the last twenty-nine has been a signalman at Farningham Road. He does his ten-hour shift with as keen a grip of his work as ever, and he looks for no reward for "just doing his duty" in saving the express. He is simply happy to know that he did the thing in the nick of time. When queried by the ubiquitous newspaper man, he said 'I did not know what had happened, for it was a very dark night, and it was so far off that I could not see what had taken place. The goods train was coming on the up-line, and for all I knew there was nothing wrong with the down-line, on which the Dover train was travelling. But it was such a curious noise that I thought there must be something wrong. Of course it does not do to stop an express train without good cause, and I might have been properly blamed if I had stopped a train for nothing. But I wanted to be on the right side. So as soon as I heard the crunching I telephoned to the next box at Swanley. I had already received warning that the express was on the way and line was clear of it.

"In another minute or two it would have been through the station and into the wrecked wagons. Fortunately, I was just in time. As soon as I heard the noise I shouted to the porter who was in the yard, and sent him down the line. I told the Swanley man to send the express cautiously down the line, and to tell the driver to be sure and pull up at my 'stop' signal. He stopped her, and she came down the line slowly to my box, arriving just nine minutes after I heard the noise. By that time the porter and the driver of the goods train had let me know of the smash, and the express was sent back to London.

"If it had happened that I had not heard the noise – the windows of my box were closed, so it was lucky I heard it – and if the express had come on through the station and dashed into the trucks near the viaduct, nothing would have saved her. She must have been hurled over the embankment."

The arrival of the railway brought an unusual and unforeseen phenomenon to Kent, illegal prize-fighting. Whilst no evidence exists to suggest that such events took place at Farningham Road itself, trains certainly passed through here on their way to secret destinations further down the line. Wealthy Londoners, the fighters themselves and hundreds of spectators would charter trains and arrive at clandestine venues where a ring was hastily constructed. In was a continual struggle for the police to prevent such events taking place as, should there be any indication that a bout had been discovered, the driver would simply be instructed to continue to another selected location. The railway company encouraged these highly profitable excursions and drivers and employees were instructed not to cooperate with the police. In 1866 three constables were badly injured by an angry crowd when they tried to stop a fight near Longfield.

As early as 1906 Farningham Road was being cited in guide books as the starting point for many rambles in north Kent and it became a popular destination with Londoners keen to escape the metropolis, especially on summer Sundays.

During World War I, Farningham Road received ambulance trains from Dover Marine. The line between Fawkham and Farningham Road operated as single line working until casualties had been removed from the trains on the up line platform. It is unclear as to where exactly they were taken but it is thought to have been to the Mabledon Hospital in Dartford.

On the morning of 16th May 1919, children and staff from the school in Horton Kirby met at the station, lining the platform to pay their respects as a train carrying the body of Edith Cavell passed through. Nurse Cavell had been executed by the Germans four years earlier for helping

No. 31662 waits in the signal box sidings prior to taking the Gravesend West service in March 1953.
R. C. Riley / Transport Treasury

allied soldiers escape occupied Belgium.

In 1934 special trains ran through Farningham Road taking large numbers of fruit pickers from London to special camps, one of which was near Longfield. In September of that year over 5 cwt of blackberries were consigned to a Mr Lamb of Bradford!

The Dartford Chronicle reported a fire in June 1938: "On Thursday night the Horton Kirby fire brigade were called to Farningham Road station, a fire having broken out in a building used as a mess-room and tool stores. The brigade were quickly on the scene, but all efforts to save the building, which was built of tarred wood and sleepers, were in vain.'

The station was narrowly missed during the Second World War when a damaged German Dornier, with parts of its wing and an engine falling off, jettisoned its bombs as it followed the railway from the Rabbits Farm area, before crashing and exploding in a field near the station where the nursery now stands. As mentioned elsewhere, the goods yards at Farningham Road were used in the war to house the wagons containing materials and heavy lifting gear to be

used in the event of air raid damage to the line. Lord Haw-Haw is recorded as having stated in one radio broadcast that the Luftwaffe intended to bomb the viaduct. German bombers attempted the target and failed. Italian Prisoners of War, housed in camps in Ship Lane, worked on clearing vegetation from the embankments – the last time it has been cleared.

The 1950s saw platforms being extended at the station and the introduction of colour light signalling. In 1964 Miles Druce Steel Limited, (later Steelstock and Corus), were given permission to establish a steel stockholder's yard with warehouses, stock, bays, offices and maintenance departments on the former goods yards adjoining the station.

Passenger services on the line from Farningham Road to Gravesend West ceased in August 1953, but the track continued with freight until March 1968, although since 1959 the line had become single track. Large stretches of its length were utilised from the A2 at Northfleet to Fawkham Junction to carry Channel Tunnel Rail Link services, which ceased in late 2007.

Being only 20½ miles from Victoria, Farningham Road was inevitably instrumental in the expansion of the villages as semi-rural retreats for commuters. The 40-minute journey to London made the area attractive and led to the dramatic growth in the 1940s, 50s and 60s of South Darenth, Sutton-at-Hone and, perhaps to a lesser degree, Horton Kirby.

Services at the station, despite what people might think, have never been as numerous as they are today. At the station's inception there were five trains daily, although it's worth noting that on the official opening date, in December 1860, the very first train broke down between Farningham Road and Meopham, leaving passengers stranded for two and a half hours. Timetables from 1943 show that Farningham Road was served on weekdays by fifteen down trains a day, with an additional five to Gravesend West, three in the morning and two in the afternoon and early evening. The up line had twenty services a day, although five of these were local trains to Swanley, four of them from Gravesend West.

By 1967 service levels had increased to twenty-four weekday trains to London and a similar number going in the opposite direction. At the time of writing, there are 32 trains towards London on weekdays and 36 stopping on the down line.

PART 2 will follow shortly.

(For those who cannot wait for Part2, John Woodhead has produced privately the story of Farningham Road station. Copies are available at £6.00 + £2.00 postage. John may be contacted at: johnwoodhead4@btinternet.com

Farningham Road signal box. Originally provided with 20 levers this had been extended to 23 levers by 1909.

On the basis that we know many readers enjoy something different.....reported as a trial trip of motor coach from set No. 2004, Norwood Junction to Haywards Heath, Sunday 8 November 1936. The load was 30 loaded coal wagons plus brake van. The train was banker to Star Lane box by No. 2352. It is seen here at South Croydon at 3.56 pm. GWT/CGS collection

Taken on one of my visits to Dad's signal box at St Cross, No 34101 'Hartland' heads south towards Eastleigh and Southampton. The home and distant signals on the same post give some indication of the short block section between here at Shawford Junction on the down line (1 mile 32 chains). With the introduction of MAS from the then Eastleigh panel, St Cross ceased to be a block post from 6 November 1966 and was abolished completely, the level crossing closed and replaced by a pedestrian footbridge, from 30 March 1969.

THE LAST STEAM AGE FIREMAN

Roger Andrews

In 1962 Roger Andews started at Eastleigh Shed as a cleaner.
His was to be a brief sojourn on the railway, progressing to fireman
before leaving for differing pastures.
As such he is well qualified to recall his memories as
one of the last steam age firemen.

It was usually a Saturday or Sunday afternoon (assuming Dad was on duty) that I would catch a bus to Winchester and spend an illicit few hours in his signal box. Very much against the rules of course and he could have got into serious trouble if I had ever been found there, but this never seemed to bother my Dad. Memories of those times are still very vivid in my mind: it was just like being in a jeweller's shop with all the highly polished brass work on the instrument shelf. The lever tops shone like silver and woe betide me if I didn't use the duster when pulling the levers: everything else was also clean and tidy, even the coal stove in the corner, which always seemed to be alight!

I had been at work for almost a year by now and although my wages were only £2-10/ a week (of which two-thirds went to my mum for my keep), I had saved enough money to buy myself a camera

It was while in Dad's signal box one day that I decided to try and become a locomotive fireman, this whilst photographing trains from the vantage point of the signal box, about a mile south of Winchester station on the main line at St Cross.

I never did learn any of the bell codes that rang out regularly but I was allowed to pull the levers when Dad was not too busy, which always took some doing, particularly with the distant signals. I was also allowed to open and close the crossing gates which were right outside the signal box. Being a busy signal box in those days, it really was a unique experience. When it was really busy and there was train after train on the up line and down lines the atmosphere was electric, what with the different bell codes ringing out, levers banging to and fro in the frame and one of the many telephones which always seemed to be ringing – this latter usually an enquiry from the next box up or down the line. These were Winchester City to the north and Shawford Junction to the South or it might have been control with a message about a certain train. The wooden box would shudder as a down train roared past, Dad took no notice calmly moving along the frame tapping out bell codes, or moving the levers in between writing it all down in the train register. I used to sit perched in the corner spellbound thinking to myself, "How do you learn all this?" It truly was a memorable experience and I am so glad I was able to watch it at first hand.

At the time my own job had lost its appeal while

Schoolboy trip for my brother and myself to London, seen here at Waterloo alongside No. 34053 'Sir Keith Park'. Although undated we know it must be prior to September 1958 when the engine was rebuilt.

Dad at Tunell Junction Southampton. He had started work as a lamp boy at Southmpton Central in the 1920s, before moving to Netley as a shunter in the 1930s. Here he had a serious accident and was off work for about two years. He then moved to Chandlers Ford as a Porter/ signalman pre WW2. In 1943 he moved to Tunnel Junction at Salisbury, it was while he was here that I was born at the railway cottages in Porton. He then moved back to Chandlers Ford in late 1945 as Porter / Signalman. The next move was around the late 1940s to Tunnel Junction Southampton and then in the mid 1950s to St.Cross until it closed. His final move after St Cross was as signalman at Botley.

the money was very poor. So, coming from a railway family - my grandfather had been chief telegraph linesman for the Southampton area and my brother was in the carriage works at Eastleigh – I decided to try for the footplate at Eastleigh motive power depot.

My father managed to arrange an interview for me with the shed master and for this I required two references. The only part of the interview I can remember well is the medical and the test for colour blindness, the latter consisted of looking for numbers made up of coloured dots about half an inch in diameter on a card made up of many same sized dots. I passed with ease and was then told I could start after I had worked out my notice for my present job.

So then it was that I started as a cleaner in 1961, at the time one of about nine cleaners and a charge-hand. With hindsight, this was a small group considering the number of engines based at the depot. The charge-hand was a middle-aged chap who, apart from telling us which engines to clean, we never saw. We had our own mess room at the very far end of the shed in the right hand corner, next to the sand furnace. The furnace was used to dry the sand for the engine sand boxes and so was alight 24 hours a day. The furnace itself was 10ft square and 4ft high and of brick construction. The process of drying the sand was simple, it was just piled on top and slowly baked until all the moisture had evaporated and it was dry enough to run smoothly through the pipe-work on the engines.

The mess room which was pretty grim, stood about 15ft square with a 15ft high ceiling, the whole lit by one solitary light bulb. There were benches down each side and at the far end an old stone sink with one cold water tap. I don't recall any sort of heating; so even by 1960s standards it was somewhat primitive, probably not having changed, or been decorated, since the shed had been built in 1903. Few of the cleaners used it, if the weather was reasonable we

would sit outside and eat our sandwiches or when it was cold we could go and sit by the sand furnace.

Unlike at other sheds I have heard of, we cleaners at Eastleigh were never involved in any other type of shed work. Nor were there any senior cleaners who only attended certain parts of the engine, we all just mucked in together and had a go at everything. I do remember us being a very happy bunch of lads who climbed on any part of the engine to clean it. There were only two rules, one you never went on the footplate, and we always put 'NOT TO BE MOVED' boards on each end of the engine before we started. The only equipment available to us was a mobile platform with wheels at one end and a ladder at the other end, this was used to clean the sides of the original Pacifics and also for filling their sand boxes.

We cleaned everything from 'West Countrys' to 'M7s'; there was certainly plenty to choose from. Even by this late date in the steam era Eastleigh's allocation was around 100 engines.

The charge hand gave us the number of the engine to be cleaned and then disappeared, although I suspect he must have kept an eye on us because he always appeared just as we'd finished ready to impart the number of the next one to be dealt with. Our actual cleaning kit was basic: for actual cleaning we used a very light oil and cloths called 'brownies'. When a driver and fireman went to the stores to return used cloths they were issued with two more cloths, one was new, called a 'whitey' and the other was a laundered 'whitey' called a 'brownie'; it was these latter cloths which was used for cleaning.

I remember being asked to go in one Sunday to help clean No. 30850 *Lord Nelson* which was coming to the end of its life and due to go out on a special. We did the Admiral proud that day, the engine looked fantastic when we had finished.

Engine cleaning certainly was a filthy business and with the rudimentary cleaning facilities in our mess room I used to go home pretty mucky. I shall never forget the look of horror on my Mum's face at the state I used to come home in! One day on my way home, I decided to call into a gentlemen's outfitters in Eastleigh (they were called that in those days) to buy a shirt. I duly parked my bicycle outside, marched in and bought my shirt. As I reached the door on the way out I happened to glance back and there on the highly polished pale wooden floor were two trails of oily footprints, one to the counter and one back to the door, where I now stood. A perfect imprint of my 'Tuff' boots which were all the rage at the time. The dirty look on the face of the very smartly dressed shop assistant told me all I wanted to know, like Queen Victoria years before, he was not amused. It was a long time before I showed my face in there again.

The most unusual thing to happen during my short time as a cleaner was to be involved in the bank run. One Thursday morning, around 10 o'clock, the charge-hand cleaner came to the engine we were working on and asked me and another lad of about the same build as myself to meet him at the time office in five minutes. We wandered over as instructed still with no idea at all what he wanted us for. We were met by the our charge-hand carrying a large black Gladstone- style leather bag and were told we were going to the bank to get the wages - we were to be security guards for half an hour. I remember looking at the other lad and we both grinned thinking this sounds like fun.

A few minutes later a taxi arrived to take us to the bank and we piled in, charge-hand in the front and us two in the back. If the taxi driver minded two dirty engine cleaners in the back of his taxi he didn't say anything. If we had known in advance what we were to be doing we could at least have cleaned ourselves up a bit and washed our hands. The drive along Campbell Road and then Southampton Road to the bank took just a few minutes, the actual bank being opposite Eastleigh station. We were dropped outside and duly marched in. This was a completely different world to the one we had just left, a world of hushed voices, pin-striped suits and pretty young ladies. I can vividly remember my face burning with embarrassment standing there covered in oil and muck with dirty oily brownies hanging from my overall pockets. What you must remember is that in the early 1960s, 17 year old lads from working class families did not go into banks. Banks were for rich people, the nearest we got to saving money was a couple of shillings in a Post Office savings book. We must have looked a right couple of clots standing in our mucky overalls with filthy dirty hands, eyes out like organ stops as several thousands

Another member of the family dynasty who was also a railwayman was uncle Bill Sedgewick. Bill worked the 'boxes at Bitterne and Netley and was also a relief ticket collector for the area. It was in the latter guise that I met him when we were both at Winchester City.

'Q' No. 30536 seemingly fresh from overhaul at the far end of the office block - the end of raised the coal stage road can be seen. Engines of this type were used on carriage shunting at Eastleigh from time to time. Naturally there were water columns at numerous locations around the shed - I recall one day being drenched by one these, it did not take long to become absolutely soaked considering the delivery rate was 1000 gallons per minute.

of pounds were packed into the black leather bag, neither of us having seen more than a few pounds in one place in our entire lives. The bag was soon packed, pieces of paper signed and exchanged and we were off.

Outside the bank the taxi had turned round and was waiting by the door with engine running, we climbed in and were retracing the same route as before over Campbell Road Bridge and into the loco sheds a journey all of about three minutes. Then it was "thank you lads" and back to the cleaning. I did the bank run once more during my short time as a cleaner. (They didn't always use cleaners, it just depended where the spare men were.) Looking back almost fifty years later the whole thing seems quite ludicrous, but that was just the way it was then.

No one was allowed on to footplate until aged 16 and I was already over that age when I started on the railway, so I was only cleaning for about two months and quickly went into the next batch of cleaners ready to step up and become a junior fireman.

The day after my second bank run all the cleaners over 16, five of us, were told to report to the footplate inspector at nine o'clock the following Monday morning, ready for a few days classroom instruction. The classroom

was situated the other side of the main office block alongside Campbell Road. This was progress at last.

Monday morning found us all there in a state of great excitement way and some little while before the appointed time. The inspector arrived exactly at 9.00 in his railway issue black mac and trilby hat. I cannot remember his name but he was a friendly chap, well-suited to teaching a bunch of scruffy engine cleaners the rudiments of boiling water. Before starting we were issued with two books, the first was a British Railways book 'Controlled Firing' and the second the Rule Book, I think all our hearts sank at the sight of the latter and especially the thickness of it with the number of rules it contained. As it turned out there were only a few rules to concern us at the moment.

Then it was straight down to business with a brief outline of how a steam engine worked and the duties of a fireman. The inspector explained the mysteries of controlled firing and the 'little and often' technique. Next we learnt the various parts of the locomotive, their purpose and how they worked. This started with the water gauge glasses and the importance of checking the water level in the boiler whenever we climbed on to a footplate. This was drummed into us and it became second nature: in fact if I climbed on

Another probable ex-works locomotive, No. 35008 'Orient Line'. In my time of the 15 covered roads at the shed, Nos. Nos 1 to 5 or 6 were kept for dead engines with the remainder used for operational engines. On the extreme right was a dead end covered bay, this was used mostly for maintenance on diesel shunters. As young cleaners we only ever worked day shifts. Promotion time was reasonable but nowhere near as rapid as at Nine Elms where there was a distinct shortage of staff. Compared with decades past, we also only cleaned 'what could be seen': this meant that it was only the outside motion that was dealt with. Compared also with times past there was no initiation ceremony, perhaps helped at the time I started I was slightly older and so physically a bit better built than the rest.

to a footplate today I am sure the first thing I would do would be to check the water level in the boiler!

Along with the importance of checking the level of water in the boiler, we learnt the purpose of the fusible plugs in the crown of the firebox and the dire consequences of what would happen if the water level got too low. This almost sounded like a hanging offence but in my few years as a fireman I never heard of anyone 'dropping a plug', as it was called. We then moved on to injectors, vacuum brakes, steam brakes and the blower - how this created a vacuum in the smoke box which in turn created a draught on the fire and many other things. To help us there were a lot of cross-sectioned models of things like injectors in the classroom.

We were then told about the brick arch why it was there and why an engine sometimes slips (the tractive effort being greater than the power of adhesion). He never got too technical which was a good thing, as he obviously knew the limits of the average engine cleaner, indeed for the first time in my life I was actually enjoying being in a classroom.

Next, it was preparation and disposal and the fireman's role in these tasks, plus all the equipment you had to

have on the engine: three lamps, three route discs, one gauge lamp, one flare lamp, three oil bottles, an oil feeder, a brush, a bucket, spanners, spare gauge glasses, detonators, green and red flags, set of fire irons, one rocker bar, a coal pick, and last but most importantly the firing shovel. Preparation could be a real pain sometimes because there was always a shortage of tools: many a time I have had to take tools off engines as they came on shed. The trouble was there were always plenty of other firemen looking for tools as well, rocker bars especially being like gold dust... but back to the classroom.

The following day it was a break from locomotive matters and we turned to the Rule Book, especially the one rule all firemen had to learn; Rule 55. This states that if you stop for more than three minutes at a signal the fireman must go to the signal and phone the signalman to find out what the problem is: if there was no phone he must go to the signal box to sign the train register and find out the reason for the delay from the signalman. Equally important was to make sure the signalman had put a collar over the appropriate signal lever as a reminder that the train was waiting.

Eastleigh West signal box, situated at the south end of the station. It was to here that our request via the train-describer would arrive ready for the appropriate road to be set for departure from the shed.

There was actually a lot more to it than that but it is still as clear in my mind today as it was all those years ago. Naturally we covered a lot more than just Rule 55, but that was the one we had to know off by heart. From memory I think we spent about three days in the classroom so we must have gone back to cleaning for the rest of the week.

The next week we did our practical experience out on the main line with an experienced crew, my duty being on the Fawley tanker train. The first morning I signed on about 8 a.m. and met the crew. We prepared our engine which was a 'midland tank' as we called them, more accurately one of the 41-thousand breed. Next we then coupled up to another midland tank (which had one of my cleaning mates on board), then we both headed for the shed exit. When leaving the shed there was a large wooden cabinet by the dummy signal at the shed exit, in this cabinet was an instrument with a large clock face type dial but only one hand. However, instead of numbers around the face there were destinations, like 'up main', 'down main', 'platform one', 'platform two', 'platform three' etc. In fact anywhere we might wish to go within the station area. By each destination was a small lever, one of which was out of its locked position indicating where the last engine to depart had gone. To start the hand moving you first pushed the lever back in and the hand would start to move, when it got to where you wanted to go, in our case Eastleigh East yard, you moved

the corresponding lever and the hand would stop. This was then repeated in the West signal box opposite on a duplicate clock face and so informed the signalman where we wanted to go. With the route set for the required destination the signalman would then pull off the ground signal when it was safe to proceed.

We ran light engine to the East yard ready to pick up our train of empty oil tanks which had come down overnight from Bromford Bridge. I was told that two tank engines were used because tender engines were not allowed over the Fawley branch due to weight restrictions.

One amusing thing about leaving the loco shed was that you could get the dummy off and start to move only to seemingly be confronted by a London bound express roaring under Campbell Road bridge on the 'up main'. Just as a collision seemed inevitable you would veer away on another line. The first few times this happened to me as a young fireman I was terrified, but you soon got used to this occurrence.

The duty was straightforward; we took the train of empty tanks down to Fawley where we had about an hour to spare. We had a bite to eat and a can of tea, then took a train of full oil tanks back to Eastleigh East yard. After this is was back light engine to the shed. I had a wonderful week, my first time on the main line, the crew were nice and friendly and as the week progressed I was allowed to do the

Eastleigh shed arrival and departure roads - right foreground - the 'L12' running south on the Portsmouth line. (Yes it really is a Southern scene notwithstanding the prominence of Great Western 'toplight' stock in the background. The cabinet with our describer stood between the shed roads and the down main line. (Taken a few years before my time at Eastleigh it is worth including as the engine is fitted to burn oil.)

firing. I was even allowed to pick up and drop off the single line token for the branch line, I learnt a lot which of course was the object of the exercise.

The following Monday was the big day when we were to be tested by Mr. Townroe the shedmaster, I was so full of information I felt like I was about to burst. In the end it was all a bit of an anti-climax, I was only asked one question on engine matters and that was 'what is the brick arch for?' which only required a simple answer, 'to aid combustion'. Then we were tested on the rules. Mr Townroe was very thorough, I had to explain Rule 55 and recite it word for word, it was a good job I had learnt it so well! After about fifteen minutes he seemed quite satisfied, and that was it, I was a passed cleaner, never to go cleaning again. The good thing about Eastleigh was that due to staff shortages once you had passed you never went back to cleaning.

Notwithstanding having passed both the theory and written tests, it was still about three months before I finally took my place on the bottom rung, the ash pan gang, and officially became a fireman. In the meantime we became a sort of 'junior spare' involved in local shunting jobs plus preparation and disposal work. The shunting jobs were varied and included: carriage works shunter, loco works shunter, Eastleigh East yard and carriage shunter, plus a few local trips to Southampton Terminus with a bit of shunting thrown in at Bevois Valley and Northam.

I clearly remember being sent down to Redbridge to spend a week on the engine at the works where sleepers and telegraph poles were 'pickled' in huge pressurised cylinders using creosote. The smell was overpowering so much so you could almost cut the air with a knife.

But my favourite shunting job was on the B4 at Winchester. In those days there was a big enough goods yard at Winchester to keep the engine shunting all day: it even had its own engine shed. I used to sign on at Eastleigh loco shed just after 7.00 in the morning and meet up with my driver, a lovely old chap who was permanently booked to that turn for health reasons and we then travelled as passengers to Winchester.

The B4 was always in steam when we arrived. It never occurred to me to ask how this was achieved - I was to find out eventually. Indeed a year later I had the night turn to light the B4 up which very nearly ended in disaster, but more of that anon.

The goods yard was on the Stockbridge Road side of Winchester station, now all given over as part of the station car park. Our job was to shunt trains that had been left in the yard and also to make up trains, plus take off or add vans to trains in the station. Consequently we spent a lot of time waiting to cross the main lines to get to the sidings on the other side of the station. In all it was a good turn for a young passed cleaner as the fire needed very little attention, the firebox on the B4 being very small. But like most inexperienced young firemen, to me I thought I was on the equivalent of a London bound express and always seemed to have too much fire on so the engine was always blowing off steam. That is until that nice old driver had a quiet word in my ear, "don't put so much coal on son, we only potter up and down the yard all day". He must have had the patience of a saint because he only ever had a constant stream of complete novice firemen to work with.

The thing that surprised me most was that all the

Winchester City from the south end. The main yard may just be seen on the left - on the 'B4' we would spend the majority of our time in this yard whilst also crossing to the down sidings at the far end of the station - that is when traffic conditions allowed!

braking was done with the hand brake which took a bit of getting used to. At first the tendency was to wind it on too hard or too quick and so stop short or lock the wheels. You certainly had to learn to anticipate what was going to happen, although after a few days you soon got the hang of it with just a gentle rub of the brakes usually enough. Certainly it was a very well-oiled hand brake.

At the end of my first day I had to throw the fire out, the engine then parked back in the shed. It was then that I leant a fireman came up from Eastleigh every night to light it up again. I certainly enjoyed my couple of weeks at Winchester, it was great to watch all the main line trains going through especially if there were a lot of boat trains each of which carried a headboard from the respective shipping line. Even so after two weeks I was glad to move on.

Another turn which I always enjoyed was the Eastleigh East yard shunter. Once on this duty I booked on at 6.00 a.m. and found my driver, a nice chap by the name of Ken. We found our engine, an 80xxx series tank engine which we had to prepare. Once this was done we ran light to Eastleigh East yard, and were into the shunting straight away. The fire and boiler required very little attention, a good fill up of coal being enough to last for hours. After a couple of hours of backwards, forwards and 'knocking off', Ken asked if I would like to have a go at driving? I have to admit I was very apprehensive to begin with, but under his guidance I soon started to get the hang of it. Like most things it was all about practice and having confidence, especially in the shunter's hand signals, about taking up the slack in the couplings, and being very careful with the

brake. All the British Railways standard types had very good steam brakes and it was all too easy to be heavy-handed and pick up the wheels, but by the end of the shift I was well into the job.

The next day and after an hour or so, Ken asked if I was alright to take over again. I was a bit taken aback but agreed straight away, Ken disappeared, I presumed to the shunters' cabin. He would just re-appear periodically to see how I was getting on. For the rest of the week I had the time of my life doing most of the driving, I shall always be grateful to Ken for having the confidence in me.

My reward for doing most of the driving was also being allowed to drive back to the loco shed after each shift, thus under Ken's guidance I soon learnt the route back to the loco shed. For this I had to learn the position of three dummies (ground signals) through the station. Being allowed to drive this short distance was a wonderful experience for a seventeen year old and it did so much for my confidence.

I had another week with a young driver whose name was Ron Finch: he was another great mate to be booked with. We booked on late afternoon and prepared our engine, another midland tank. We then went off shed and ran light to Eastleigh carriage sidings to pick up four carriages which we then took to the station to await our passengers. We left about 5.30 p.m. and ran down to Southampton Terminus stopping at Swaythling, St. Denys and Northam.

Southampton Terminus was a very busy station in those days, and it was here we spent the rest of our shift doing the odd bit of shunting, after which we then ran light engine back to Eastleigh. It was about this time I had an encounter with a man of opposite type, a very miserable driver, I was sent to work with him on the carriage shunter at Eastleigh station. He was actually a main line man who had come in late and missed his turn which had in consequence put him in a very bad mood. We walked to the station and found our engine, this time an 'M7', a type I had never worked on one before, largely because there were few left by this time. As a result I had to ask the driver to show me where the water and steam feeds were for the injectors, this made his bad mood even worse. It was not helped when I could not get the actual injectors to work. For him this was the last straw as he proceeded to ridicule and humiliate me in front of the carriage shunters, not a very pleasant experience. But this sort of behaviour was very rare, in fact it was the only time I encountered such an attitude in my time on the railways.

There was also one occasion which ended in a very unpleasant experience. I was on the loco works shunter with an elderly driver who was permanently on shunting duty. This particular morning it was very foggy. As usual we had a midland tank which we prepared. Our instructions from the running foreman were that instead of leaving the shed by the normal route we had to go off shed the back way which took us out on to the Portsmouth line.

Having prepared our engine we prepared to set off. Unfortunately we could not go back through the shed because all the roads were blocked by engines, so the plan was to go almost as far as Campbell Road bridge on the normal exit road, then cross over on to the incoming road and go down over the blow down pit, which was the first stop for all engines coming on shed. In this way we would bypass the turntable and go down the Campbell Road side of the main office block and also allow us to avoid the engines on the disposal pits. We could then exit out the back way as planned.

Thus for the first stage we left the shed on the normal exit road almost as far as Campbell Road bridge where we stopped ready for me to get down and change the points to reverse over to the incoming road. This was also a day of thick fog, so thick I could hardly make out the actual bridge. I changed the points and started to climb back on the footplate, as I did so I shouted "alright mate" and my driver started to move back over the crossover. I climbed aboard and stuck my head out of the window only to see that a few feet from our engine was a 9F 2.10.0 creeping towards the shed through the murk - and we were passing right in front of it. I tried to shout a warning but nothing came out, I was struck dumb with fright. It would have made no difference anyway, a collision was inevitable. There was an almighty bang which must have been heard all over the shed with our engine knocked clean off the rails. The 9F hit us broadside, right in the middle of the side tank as we crossed its bows. The side tank was badly holed and in consequence all the water was pouring out. The driver of the 9F seemed to think

I should have seen him, in truth I should have done, but he must have appeared in the few seconds it took me to climb on board and stick my head out of the window.

As is usual in these circumstances, within a few minutes there were a dozen people present including the running foreman. My driver, who had said very little since the incident and myself were told to go back to the shed and take another midland tank which was already prepared and carry on with our turn. There was no 'how are you?' or 'are you alright to continue?', we just had to get on with our shift.

This time we found our way out through the back of the shed and so carried on with our turn. The derailment must have caused chaos for a few hours as the shed entrance was blocked, but by then we were out of sight in the loco works. When our shift ended the fog had lifted and it was a beautiful sunny day. We came back to the shed on the usual approach road with no sign at of the incident at all, everything having been cleared away. I was very worried for some days in case I was held responsible or blamed in some way, but I never heard another word about it.

To be continued

Fawley, August 1964. Andrew Muckley

Having looked at differing styles and body widths in the previous two files, in this issue we will look at the various types of passenger coaches built. Leaving aside catering vehicles, the Southern under Maunsell, unlike some of its contemporaries, confined itself essentially to nine types for steam stock. Variations within a type were largely in style, width and in minor interior differences.

These nine types (all corridor) were:

8-compartment 3rd	Open Third	General saloon (unclassed)
6-compartment Brake 3rd	4-compartment Brake 3rd	Nondescript Brake (unclassed)
6 compartment-Brake Composite	7-compartment 1st	7-compartment Composite

The Southern did not build any new non-corridor steam stock.

*Here we see **S4097S, an example of a 'long' Brake 3rd with 4 compartments** built for services where passengers were expected to have a large amount of luggage. This vehicle is one of a batch of 27 high window 'Restriction 4' coaches built to diagram 2101 in 1929. 28 similar vehicles but with low windows, had previously been built to R4 together with four for R1. No. 4097 was one of a number built for through services to other companies and was allocated to the 'Sunny South Express'. It subsequently became a loose vehicle but in June 1954 was formed into 8-set No. 469, a special traffic set allocated to Blackheath. Withdrawn in June 1961 it is seen here at Newhaven on 7 August 1961 awaiting breaking up.*

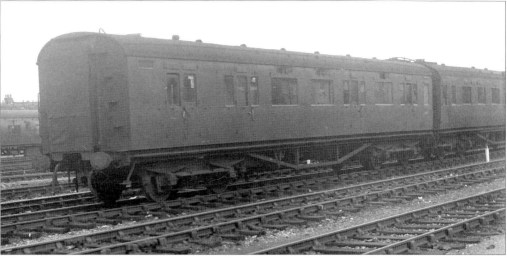

Right - Nondescript saloon Brake No. S4431S is pictured at Eardley on 17 August 1960. It was the first of 20 similar vehicles built in 1933 to diagram 2654 for Continental Boat services. A loose vehicle, it was 8ft 6in wide (and therefore Restriction 1) which gave a wide route availability. This was a new design not seen previously with a centre gangway and two 'armchair' seats one side and one the other. They were similar inside to the General Saloons, but the exterior appearance was different and distinctive. With such plush seating they could be designated 1st 2nd or 3rd class as necessary. In the early 1960s most (including No. 4431 which was briefly in set No. 212) were allocated to special traffic sets. It was withdrawn in June 1961.

*Above - A clear view of the corridor side of **6-compartment 3rd Brake S4239S** shows the final flowering of Maunsell's design. Note the clear functional lines and the huge windows extending to the cantrail. No. 4239 was one of 20 brake vehicles for 3-sets Nos. 952 – 961 built in 1936 to Diagram 2113 and allocated to the South Eastern section. Apart from a sliding door replacing a hinged one between the guard's and passenger accommodation and the external doors being between compartments instead of in front of alternate ones, Diagram 2113 is dimensionally exactly the same as No. 2102 to which the very first Maunsell 6-compartment brakes had been built 10 years previously. The exterior appearance is, however, light years away. Seen here at Salisbury on 18 August 1962 it was withdrawn at the end of the year. This design was perpetuated for a couple of years in electric stock but no more Maunsell steam stock was built. [All photos David Wigley]*

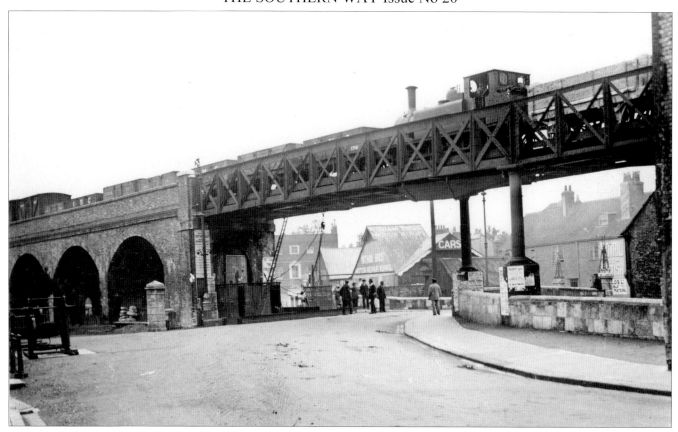

OVER and UNDER

Something that has been gathering dust within the 'To be Used' box(es) has been this selection of bridge views from the Southern system. (There are others as well.) On the basis that they can now be enjoyed by not just me, a small selection, but I will admit with only limited information as per what is (or is not) on the reverse of the prints.

Opposite top - *The long forgotten Sandown line viaduct at Newport, reported as taken in 1920. A number of the wagons display the initial 'IWC', in the background is 'Witham Bros. Motor Repair Works'.*

Opposite bottom - *Still on the IOW but this time a Cowes line train on the viaduct north of Newport. No date or other details, but credited to Michael P Jacobs.*

Above - *The impressive girder structure at Shalford Junction south of Guildford. In the background the Portsmouth line may be seen running left to right, the train approaching reported as the 12.02 from Guildford. Interestingly there is no check rail within the running rails and instead this is provided on the outsides.*

Page 70, top - *'C' class No. 31724 piloting an unidentified 'Mogul' on the combined 3.20 pm Tonbridge - Redhill goods plus on a empty ballast train for Edenbridge. The view was taken on the Tonbridge to Redhill route which crosses the Oxted line west of Edenbridge.* Derek Cross

Page 70, bottom - *The old Redbridge viaduct west of Southampton. 'U' No. 31639 with a ballast train. From the flimsy appearance of the structure it is hard to believe this is, in fact, part of the Bournemouth main line. 21 May 1962.*
Michael J Fox

Page 71 - top - *The canal bridge at New Cross Gate, December 1962.*

Page 71, bottom - *Crossing the River Adur (at high tide), Shoreham-by-Sea. 'Q' No. 30533 with a Brighton to Lancing freight, 14 October 1962.* S Creer.

Opposite top - *'K' class No. 32352 on the 3.28 pm Haywards Heath to London Bridge, crossing Cooks Pond Bridge at Dormans.*

Opposite bottom - *Into Hampshire now, with 'Schools' No 30929 'Malvern' approaching Fareham with a Brighton to Bournemouth working. 14 June 1962.* *J Cupit*

Above - *The opposite side of the same structure (this the largest rail viaduct in Hampshire). On 1 November 1961, 'D15' No. 30470 has just left Fareham, Portsmouth bound with a service from Bristol.*

P M Alexander

To conclude, three views from the West Country. **Above** - Bere Ferres, no details of locative or train but from the headcode a main line working. **Opposite top** - No prizes for recognising Meldon, a '75xxx' Standard 4 with an Exmouth Junction to Plymouth Friary freight. The amount of revenue from just three wagons would certainly not cover the running costs of the train let alone the overheads associated with the route traversed. Finally**, opposite bottom**, the legacy of reduced traffic. The Ilfracombe line viaduct at Barnstaple over the river Taw. Seen here out of use and awaiting eventual demolition. In the meanwhile it affords a useful vantage point for those wishing to 'dangle their maggots' D Doble. **Right** - A reminder of days past at Barnstaple...

We are somewhat humbled this time with some appreciated positive comments, but before relaying these I must admit an error. Several have pointed out Ryde (SW19) is in fact Gravesend. My fault, yet again do not believe what is written on the reverse without having checked first. (Thanks to Dick Metcalfe-Thomes, Stephen Lacy, David Lindsell, Viv Orchard and others.)

But now to the plaudits - "Another excellent issue Kevin! As a member of the Colonel Stephens Society, I especially appreciated the three items in SW 18 which, in their different ways, feature Robertsbridge - especially that magnificent double spread of the railmotor. But I want to respond to your conundrum about the V signs on the luggage compartment ends of the DEMUs. I remember when the DEMUs came in, replacing T9s etc., on local trains through Fareham. At some point the Vs were painted a fluorescent orange. But when the small yellow panels became nearly universal throughout BR, a black inverted triangle was introduced, again at the luggage/guard's compartment ends. But this was not confined to DEMUs. See the 2BIL illustrated on page 25 of SW 18. We also understood that it was to indicate to station staff the location of the luggage compartment. But it would not be much use when two or more units were coupled together. I hope someone else can solve this minor mystery. Ross Shimmon Editor 'The Colonel'"

The final resting place of Star Lane crossing box and also the topic of the 'V' on the Hampshire units has created much interest. Firstly from Julian Clark, "Star Lane Box now resides at Bill McAlpine's private Fawley Hill Railway, Nr. Henley on Thames, Oxon. Your conjecture that it may not have travelled far from its original site is borne out by their 1994 guide book " The box was moved (by hay cart) two miles to a local garden where it was used as an aviary". It was (presumably) moved from this site to Fawley in 1987. I am sure that Sir William McAlpine (or his curator!!) would be able to provide further info.

"I had always assumed that the 'V' on the brake car on a Thumper was the predecessor of the triangle, and that the triangle was a logical inversion of the V when yellow visibility panels were introduced, then becoming a generic indicator, spreading to EMUs. It would be interesting to keep an eye on photos of units from that period to have an idea of when it appeared to have been introduced. A new preoccupation for the next little while ! I don't recall seeing a 'V' on any unit other than the Hampshires; I don't think I have seen them on an Oxted unit ,only the triangle.

"Michael Welch has stated in several texts that the triangle was to indicate the brake end to platform staff, but it is curious to consider how and when the general usage of the indication may have developed, particularly from DEMUs to EMUs. The indication would be an irrelevance on Subs and Hastings Units where they would have been superfluous, but whether anything slipped through on a hybrid is another possible permutation.

Certainly some Tadpoles in the later Rail Blue , and then Blue/ Grey livery had them (despite the parcels car), as did Hastings unit 1003 , which I think interchanged with some Tadpoles...curious.

"David Brown who wrote the new Southern Electric Histories (Capital) attends the Chi RCTS so I'll ask him about his views when I next see him."

On a similar theme from Greg Beecroft, "Kevin, you ask where Star Lane gate box went to. I do not know if it went directly there from Wokingham, but it is at Sir William McAlpine's private railway at Fawley Hill, near Henley-on-Thames.

"With respect to the '2 Bil' article, please note that the Southern printed unit codes, for almost all types, with only the first letter upper case. The only exceptions were 'EPB' and 'DD'. Ian Allan is responsible for the incorrect use of upper case letters for other codes.

"The yellow V on the end of '3H' units was to indicate the end with the guard's van. The was principally for Post Office staff waiting to load mail bags. The black triangle on unit ends later served the same purpose. 'EPB' and 'Sub' units did not carry black triangles, even though there was a guard's van in the front carriage. This was because mail and parcels were carried in the rear van.

"Keep up the good work with Southern Way. Its nice to find a magazine that recognises that the railways were not just about steam locos but an industry that, like the military, could turn its hand to anything and everything. I formed a view many years ago that only such trades as sagger makers (and their bottom knockers) were probably not represented somewhere in the industry." - or does somebody know differently?

Now from Tony Booth - see 'Stationary Boilers' in SW19 has commented further, "Relating to the notes on the SR Stationary Boilers please note that I did not compile the list. It was done by Nick Pigott (Editor - The Railway Magazine) following some articles in the magazine. Nick is President of the **Engine Shed Society** and I am the website manager and therefore only uploaded Nick's table. Perhaps you could clarify this in your next issue". A pleasure and my apologies to both Nick and Tony. It may worth pointing out that information on the use of two Bulleid boilers as stationary plant is given in Bradley's, 'Locomotives of the Southern Railway - Part 2' - page 79.

Now from Derek Taylor on the subject gated crossings, coasting boards and shunting. (Page numbers refer to Issue No 19.) "p100 - Mr Raggetts letter refers to nine gated crossings remaining on Southern territory. I think there are two more that he hasn't mentioned , Stone C'rossing (19m 14ch) and Shornmead (27 m 01ch) on the North Kent route Stone Crossing is still manned.

"p73 - Lineside coasting boards are still part of the Network Rail infrastructure and from personal experience it is only occasionally possible to use them. They are for guidance when running to time but within the

London suburban area where the schedules are so tight it is more common to be trying to claw back lost time ! Certainly the TOC management wish to reduce the electricity bill and score environmental brownie points and do from time to time remind drivers about using coasting boards.

"p74 - The shunting movement with the guard "riding shotgun" still occurs today at Strood in order to avoid the driver from having to climb out into the cess to change ends . 8 car trains depart down the Medway Valley line until clear of the crossover. The driver is then able to bring the train back into the station ."

Terry Hastings, the Assistant Operating Manager for the Isle of Wight Steam Railway (...thinking aloud here I must be overdue for a visit...), sends some most interest comments on SW18 and Jim Gosden's notes on IOW Guards as appeared on P71. "For a couple of years towards the end of steam working on the Island I became familiar with a few of the local guards. Being a new, young railwayman myself these chaps were quite forthcoming about their approach to the job.

"Most of the more agile guys were happy to board moving trains - not as an affectation but more as a matter of practicality. The necessity was driven by a number of factors,

curved stations, tight timetables and a constant flow of mail from general offices to stations, there were other factors as I shall show.

"A Ventnor road train was about 390ft long in the summer months and filled the full length of the platforms. At a steady pace it took about 65 seconds to walk its length.

"Island working generally placed a van at each end of the train but inevitably station entrances, where staff were certain to be, were located mid-way down the platform. Upon arrival the guard may have walked at least half way down the train to pass over small mail. Whilst in the area he would check doors and if necessary open First Class compartments. (Island practice was to keep 1st Class locked). His other station duties would include loading/unloading the van, and operating the Stones lighting pull-rod switches at stations before and after tunnels...one switch per vehicle, a walk the full length of the train. All of these functions take time, a commodity the Island timetable had very little of, especially in the summer.

"To speed matters along, many guards became adept at giving the right-away some distance from the van, letting the train come to them thus saving precious seconds.

"The process was not particularly difficult provided

Regular readers will know we are always on the look for the unusual to include in SW. Please, absolutely nothing wrong with the 'norm' but as example how often would the above have been likely to occur? It was taken at Basingstoke on 12 September 1954 and shows N15X No. 32328 'Hackworth' shunting a former LNER beaver-tail observation car, once part of the famous 'Silver Jubilee' train set. I suspect some may already have worked out how and why, but for all others it was all part of the Farnborough Air Show of that month. (Whilst being fortunate to have access to almost a full set of Special Traffic Notices for the 1950s, the few that are missing cover the period July to December 1954, so unfortunately no further details so far. Hopefully someone can supply the missing pieces.)

you took a firm hand-hold on the commode handle and transferred your body weight from the platform to the running board at exactly the same moment! It helped if the door was left on the swing (most I.W. vans had outward opening doors in the 50s & 60s and some stock which had run on the mainland with inward opening doors were specially converted to outward opening upon transfer.) Sticky varnish on a recent ex-shops vehicle could sometimes cause a problem for a day or two but it just meant one had to leave the handle in the closed position so the door could not shut.

"As a matter of interest, five car bogie formations are regularly run on the Isle of Wight Steam Railway although guards there have a much easier life; their biggest problem is the modern customer who fails to understand the use of the door handle…expecting doors to open AND close automatically. With about 35 – 40 doors in each train there is a fair bit of walking to keep them all in check.

"Although not permitted under safety rules I.W. guards still need to sight the driver on curved platforms walking at least half the train's length to give the tip. Nowadays there is a brief pause to allow the guard to return to the van before the off. (Sadly this allows those who have mastered the door handle time to open them after the right-away is given!) So much for safety rules. One guard, who shall remain nameless, has been reprimanded for perpetuating the ways he learnt in the early '60s …old habits die hard!"

Now from David Vidler, "In 'Rebuilt' (SW19), you say that Dave Waldron thought that the photograph used as the frontispiece to SW15 showed 21C1 on the Westbury line at Salisbury. It is in fact on the GWR exchange siding between the SR and GWR running lines and is almost certainly about to shunt its train into the GWR Fisherton Yard after arriving from Eastleigh as indicated by the headcode. The photograph was published in the January 1942 issue of 'Railway Magazine' where it is incorrectly captioned as 'a heavy goods train leaving Salisbury'. The train is probably a mid-morning freight from Eastleigh to the GWR which was used for trial trips of the Merchant Navies in 1941."

On a totally separate tack, John Lacy reports, "I am pleased you decided to include the pre 1948 memories of Bill Trigg, above all the railways were a human run system and off the railway, of the participants often influenced they way things were done and bring the railway to life.

Being, possibly, a bit more old fashioned than you - coming of age occurs at 21, not 18 !! - *yes I know but we have to promote ourselves a bit!*

"On the matter of BILs (and HALs) it was a standard practice when snow fell to keep these in 8-car formations for the Mid Sussex and Seaford lines simply because the number of collector shoes would plough their way along. It was a bit rough on the Gatwick services though, as their units carried on south instead of being detached for the return working from Gatwick to Victoria. CIGs and VEPs with the lighter shoe gear could from be pretty useless in snow and ice conditions as they amply demonstrated.

"You could always tell when one of the BILs, HALs and LAVs unit was suffering from old age if you travelled in the guard's van. The van had six major surfaces: four walls, floor and ceiling plus four doors in pairs on each side of the train. Once the train got up any speed each of the six major

Colin Chivers, (South Western Circle), has forwarded the below plus the accompanying image, any suggestions would be welcome..

"It was taken inside either Strood or Higham tunnels in the late 1950s or very early 1960s. My Grandfather, Edward Butcher who is seen here holding the pole against the measuring board, was latterly ganger for the 3 mile section through both tunnels until his retirement on 28 September 1962. My mother thinks it was taken in Strood tunnel (always the more problematic) after a fall of chalk from the unlined roof. None of the other men in the view are known but my mother again believes that one of them is the District Engineer who signed his retirement certificate (framed and displayed on our spare bedroom wall). Unfortunately his signature is not very clear – may be 'Prior'.

"I have no idea about what they are doing – perhaps your tame PW guru could enlighten us even if you decide the picture is too poor to use in SW."

surfaces, plus the four doors, would start to develop a motion independent of each adjoining surface and could, for the faint hearted, induce a form of sea-sickness. The faster the train's speed, the greater the independence of the motions. But, as they say, there's more. Each of those 10 surfaces (objects) was made of planked timber and each plank of timber also took on a motion independent of its neighbours! The 4-LAV sets were the worst.

"Page 71 - Vee is for Van. This is not a conundrum, nor is it a matter for dispute or argument. It is nothing whatsoever to do with the later yellow (safety) ends but everything to do with time keeping. The Southern (whether it be Railway or Region) worked in quarter minutes - none of your Prideaux - inter city inspired "if its less than 10 minutes late its on time" here! The Vee mark was there to tell the staff which end the guard's van was. Consider - 20 second dwell time allowed unless longer was shown in the WTT. If you are at the wrong end of the train when it comes to a stand and have to trundle the sack barrow or parcel trolley to the other end, fighting your way through the passenger streams moving at right angles to your own trajectory as you go, your 20 seconds has already long gone before you start loading or unloading. The markings were essentially confined to 3 car DEMUs because pretty well everything else had a van at both ends of the set. The 'first final solution' was to put the guard's van in the middle (CIG/BIG) so the van would be within feet of the platform staff regardless. The 'second final solution' came later - we stopped carrying parcels and letter mails and abolished the guard's van altogether.

"Talking of CIG/BIG stock, the description stood officially for Corridor/Buffet Intermediate Guard ('s van). The fact that IG was the telegraphic code for Brighton has nothing to do with it of course! Pure coincidence! And still on these sets, have you ever had to manually apply or take off the electric parking brake on the mark 1 series? If you have, you'd fully applaud that the later builds reverted to traditional hand brakes and why they never ran on the south western side."

Now a justified correction from Stuart Hicks, "Another fascinating read thank you. On page 19, (SW Special Issue No 8) the 4EPB shown on the down line is a SR type (5001-5260) and therefore is not 5360 which was of the BR standard design (with a cleaner roof and in particular no longitudinal cable runs)."

David Lindsell takes us to task re P32 of Issue 19, "The picture on page 32 shows a Horsham train not one to Brighton. I used to travel to Bramber quite a lot as a lad in the 1950's as my Grandparents lived in Roman Road, Steyning and Bramber was the nearest station to their home. We took an electric train from our local station at Fratton, usually formed of 2-BIL or 2-HAL units, to Shoreham changing into the Horsham Push-Pull which was worked either by an M7 or H tank. I can understand the comments of Nicholas Owen as I have a lasting memory of riding the old electric units."

From Viv Orchard although unrelated to his p/way image, "SW 19 page 59 and Horsham shed. The attached is a

Derek Taylor has sent the attached image, comments would be welcome. "A while back in conversation I mentioned that I had an old chair that only has two-bolts instead of the usual three on the Southern. I've finally got round to photographing it . I don't know if this is of any interest for your p-way articles in Southern Way ." (Apologies for nothing on p/way of late. Graham will be back, just pressure of work on his part for the present.)

As speaking of p/way, this from Viv Orchard, "On the Southern, on seldom used points, the crossing was often sprung such that the normal running line did not have a gap in it. For the other route the wheel flange forced the crossing over against the spring. Such items existed at Horsley, Clandon and London Road Guildford and one still exists on the Isle of Wight. However, I was surprised to see the same item in use on Vancouver Island! I had thought they were a Southern or LSWR item only. Does anyone have further info on these?"

On the first day of public service with the new Oxted DEMU units, 16 June 1962. No. 1304 leaves Heathfield tunnel with the 12.45 pm Eastbourne to Tunbridge Wells service. (- and not a 'V' or yellow end to be seen!)

later version showing some of the inhabitants. I am a member of the Londondon Vintage Taxi Association and as a result a fellow member from Penrith area but staying on the Isle of Wight contacted me. It turned out he was a Passed Fireman at Horsham and regularly worked the line to Guildford. He stated the first train in the morning to Guildford was rare in that the engine was in the centre of the Push & Pull train. The first job was to go to the end of a siding and attach a single Push & Pull coach. The engine would then run to the other end of the siding and attach a two-oach Push & Pull Set plus a Control Van. The whole would then go to Guildford. The reason being that this was the London commuter train taking many people from Cranleigh and Bramley & Wonersh to Guildford for thier electric train to Waterloo. The picture on page 58 of Langston Swing Bridge signal box is interesting. It was seldom opened yet it obviously is here as the window is open. A railwayman told me years ago it was the only box that was one class from bottom on that District. It had to be opened occasionally as it was the only way of progressing through the classes of Signalman for promotion."

On the same theme of Horsham was this in a letter from John Davenport. 'Can't do an allocation for 1939, but sometime in late SR days my childish manuscript book shows:

0-6-0: 538, 540-4, 2300-09, 3445, 2550/1.
0-4-2T: 2239, 2252/5, 2283.
0-4-4T: 2370/2/3/6/, 2354-7.
0-6-2T: 2400/2, 2497, 2501/10/13/17/20, 2520/3. 2557/65.
0-6-0T: 2684.

"Page 83 - Percy. I'll have a go at this one. Lt. Col. Percy Montague Brookham-Hitching R.E. (Retd.). He was a real railway enthusiast, and knew everyone on the Southern. I suspect he is somewhere in the photo of the early Merchant Navy antics. When he went to Bournemouth on a holiday, the Waterloo Station Master was on duty to meet him. He gave me his copy of the 1948 Interchange Trails report which was inscribed on the cover as belonging to Col. Harold Rudyard, who was a very high up in the Railway Executive. I am reasonably sure he knew Missenden. So that's my useless contribution. I would add that the Colonel could get a legal footplate pass with one phone call." *John - thank you, certainly not useless, indeed far from it - Ed.*

Another query solved now thanks to Arnie Braden. In issue 19, pages 60/61 we printed a view of a steam cleaning machine, "...my early life was spent at Stewarts Lane...these machines were called 'Weavers' and the solution used was caustic soda and steam. A story I heard was that they were developed for washing the bombers of WW2 after returning from missions.

"The article on milk trains took me back to a turn at Stewarts Lane where we picked up full tanks at Kensington Olympia in the morning and returned the empties in the afternoon. There was a CWS bottling plant at the rear of SL depot, the line into the milk depot had a very sharp curve hence no big engines, in the early days they used an 0-4-0 crane engine, when this was scrapped a 'P' class 0-6-0T replaced it."

Having resolved some issues we created another and are rightly taken to task by Tony Logan, "If the caption to the photo on page 18 (SW19) is to be believed, some explaining is called for in respect of the 'sunshine' numerals on the buffer beam! Surely it is No. 3488...!" *Tony, you are of course correct, blame the Ed not the author of the article!.*

Now from Tony Carter - whose article on Steyning appeared in SW19. " I was interested in reading about milk by rail as I was born in the Station House at Seaton Junction where the Express Dairy had a depot. It opened in the late 1930s and continued for a while after the station closed in the Beeching era.

"My father was SM there and said they chose that site as there was an unending supply of water, he said a water diviner arrived with a twig! Even now water still runs down the cess from Honiton Tunnel 24 hours a day.

"On another theme, when I left Steyning, I was appointed as SM at Farningham Road. This was such an anti-climax after Steyning with its large station buildings, market, signal box in circuit all day and a busy town. Prior to me going there its main reputation was for freight train derailments from train Ferry van trains going too fast. It is said that orchards grew up alongside the track as so much fruit fell from the vans!"

Finally, concerning our Meon valley part 1 book, this from John Ambler, "Seeing the comment on Meon Valley Volume 1, photo 27 in the SW 18 letters pages, I remembered that I had forgotten to send you a comment on photo 30.

"You speculate that the location is possibly near one of the tunnel excavations, and wonder what the boy in the centre is carrying.

"My feeling is that the items that are in the hands of the "nipper" offer support for your speculation. I have seen such items in photos of Cornish tin miners. They are bundles of candles which would have been the only lighting available underground at this date.

"Candles were made by draping a wick over a rod, then dipping the two trailing ends repeatedly into molten tallow, leaving a loop of wick which was used to carry bundles just as the boy in the photo is doing.

"Really enjoyed the images in Volume 1, and looking forward to starting Volume 2." John, thank you, and indeed to all who take the trouble to email, write and phone - Ed.

The SOUTHERN WAY CATALOGUE

Alan Postlethwaite

The Southern Way Catalogue was launched on a website in August 2012. It comprises thousands of entries on hundreds of topics in 22 categories. The need for such a catalogue arose as the magazine collection became encyclopedic in size and scope. It simply took too long to find material. The catalogue covers both text and illustrations, giving the Issue and Page numbers of each entry and identifying any in colour. The intention is to update it after publication of each Issue and Special Issue. It was a challenge to read every page thoroughly to identify material that warranted an entry. As one of the few people to have reviewed *SW* as a whole, I can now offer some comments on its achievements to date and why we find its content so interesting.

Launched in January 2007, *The Southern Way* is a quality magazine which has received tremendous support from a wide variety of Southern devotees. The material is presented in an informal style, making readers feel like club members rather than subscribers. Most *SW* material is published there for the first time. Ancient photographs are much appreciated, so too are the many technical articles, covering a vast range of topics. Life stories are among the most cherished, adding personal precision to line histories, operation, construction and so forth. Prime examples of this are the Callington Branch (Issue 7) and Winchester Memories (Issue 11).

In BR days, the steam railway held a special fascination because it was largely Victorian technology operating some fifty years after the good Queen had died. I for one recognised that antiquity when I discovered the steam railway in the 1950s. There were mid-Victorian stations, locomotives from the 1870s, late Victorian signalling, Edwardian coaches, local goods traffic (especially coal), bullhead track, an abundance of friendly railway people and a dearth of passengers for much of the day. We photographed it all prolifically, sensing that modernisation and closures were imminent. Much of the old technology has been preserved in museums and on heritage lines but the old way of life has been largely lost. We are indebted to all who have contributed accounts of life on the Southern during the late steam age.

Being largely unautomated, the steam railway was prone to human error and accidents. A long list in the catalogue shows that signals were passed at danger, block systems were circumvented and guards did not always check everything that they should. Training was sometimes inadequate, exemplified by the Littlehampton porter who did not know how to connect brake pipes and connected a redundant one. Most chilling is an Inspector's comment that six mishaps in a decade is not a high rate for a station the size of Bournemouth West (Special Issue 8).

The steam locomotive was inherently difficult to drive safely, partly because of restricted forward vision and partly because operation was 100% manual with imperfect instruments and controls. False reading of a gauge glass resulted in two instances of a Lord Nelson firebox running dry (Issue 17), in one case causing a catastrophic explosion due to imperfect fusible plugs. Despite noble attempts by the LMS and LNER to introduce the (safer) water-tube boiler, the steam railway was stuck with the fire-tube shell boiler until the end. In the wrong hands, the steam locomotive was a dangerous beast but to the enthusiast, it was enthralling.

Of the eight Special Issues of *SW* to date, the three on *Wartime Southern* are particularly poignant, capturing locations that are rarely photographed and showing both the war damage and the people needed to clear the rubble and make repairs. These gangs were mostly of men beyond military age, often dressed in three-piece suits and wearing the ubiquitous flat cap. We are reminded too of the fragility of daily life during the war. Buses, trams and tubes must have been packed as all the SR London termini were closed variously for days, weeks or months. We are indebted to *SW* and all the archivists for such additional social history.

The 22 Categories:

Coaches, Sets & Units
Common Abbreviations
Contributors
Financial Topics
Freight, Parcels & Mails
Line Histories
Articles in the Magazine
Locomotives
Locomotive Facilities
Military Topics
Model railways
Operation
Other Facilities
People & Animals
Permanent Way
Publicity and Ephemera
Road Transport
Ports, Quays & Ships
Signals
Signal; Boxes
Stations
Works

Food for thought - some neglected topics:

Architecture
ARP Signal Boxes
Auxiliary signals
Brake systems
East Kent Railway
Exmouth Junction Works
Guard's life stories
Coast of Arms
London goods stations
Longhedge works
Mechanical horses
Meldon Quarry
Signal looking mechanisms
Telegraphy and bell codes
Thamside quays and piers
Tickets
Track circuitry

A few statistics:

368 magazine contributors have been identified to date. The most prolific is Terry Cole (19 issues). A close second to Terry is Graham Hatton (17 issues). The longest categories are Stations and Locomotives. The shortest categories are Finance and Model railways. One cat and a fox have found their way in to the magazine. There are two entries on Elephants and three on Guards.

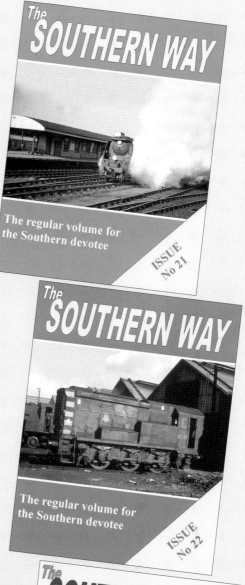

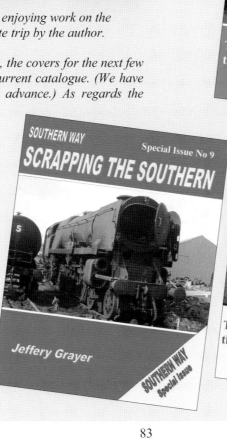

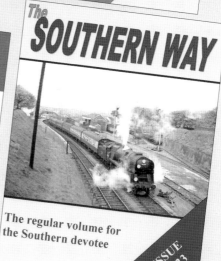

Terry Cole (left) and Martin Burch enjoying work on the Bluebell. The occasion of a footplate trip by the author.

To illustrate what is in preparation, the covers for the next few issues are shown - details in the current catalogue. (We have to prepare these some months in advance.) As regards the regular issues and their respective contents, that is more difficult, but at the time of writing, locomotives, reminiscences, rolling stock, architecture, Traffic Committee Notes, Cannon Street Signal Box fire, EMUs, headcodes, Basingstoke, Longmoor, Battersea Tangle, Chessington, Staines, Ashford, Southern diesel shunters - all are planned and will hopefully appear. Plus whatever else is offered in the meanwhile (and it is always welcome). I cannot guarantee anything further on guards, foxes or elephants, but I can promise material that will not have been seen before! - Ed.

No. 614 awaiting departure on what is clearly a special working. (We can be sure someone will know what and where!) The engines changed little over the years retaining for example the piston tail rods, a feature which went out of fashion elsewhere. Several similar views of differing engines on special workings exist - a clue might have been the decorative disc and the similar item being carried by the man on the extreme right. Unfortunately neither can be clearly identified.

The 'J' CLASS ENGINES OF THE SE&CR

A Small Band of Brothers

David Austin

The 20th Century was a new start for the South Eastern & Chatham Railway. During the last half of the 1800s the company had been in a state of perpetual flux and had to cope with the competition of neighbouring railway companies, increasing traffic demands and an uncompromising travelling public. The rail pathways into London from the south-east were limited to just one line of way through London Bridge station and as a consequence, congestion was a constant problem. The situation was not helped by a personal animosity between Edward Watkin and James Forbes, respectively the chairmen of the South Eastern (SER) and the London, Chatham & Dover, (LC&D) railways. The competition between the two men added to the general mayhem as both railways felt obliged to construct unwanted, and at times unaffordable routes.

At the end of the 1800s the SER may have captured the prestigious Continental traffic, and with it the glamorous and fast running trains, but the local residents had good reason to hate the company. The London commuting fraternity in the northern suburbs of Kent were not as slow as their trains in coming forward to air their complaints in the national newspapers. The frequent refrain of unpunctuality, high fares and third-class carriages spoke volumes of a company under pressure from the travelling public and falling behind the competition of new inner city transport systems.

The South Eastern Railway (SER) came into being for the sole purpose of establishing a line of communication from London to Paris with a cross-channel boat link to connect the two railway systems. In the mid-1800s the SER built a main line from London towards the Kent coast with the aim of developing this service to the Continent. The line ran eastwards from London Bridge following the route of the London and Greenwich Railway and turning south at Corbetts Lane to New Cross and Croydon. A westwards extension to serve the City (Cannon Street) and West End (Charing Cross) was opened in 1865. The route ran to Ashford, including a branch to Maidstone, Folkestone, and eventually reaching Dover in 1844. The SER opened their station at Folkestone harbour in 1843 and, having established an arrangement with the New Commercial Steam Packet Company for steamer services to Boulogne, had opened up a new and lucrative market. The cross-channel ferry service was the final link in a line of

The same engine in photographic grey. Built in December 1913 it had a service life a few months under 36 years.

Complete with Southern 'A' prefix and what appears to be, the SECR cast plate on the bunker on the bunker. Notice too the works plate on the front splashier. The family resemblance with the 'H' class tank is also apparent.

communication which connected London, the capital of the Empire, with the main capitals of Europe. The service established the world's first rail-sea-rail transport system, whilst in later years it formed part of a useful link for the Indian and eastern mails traffic. The best engines and most luxurious carriages were reserved for this prestigious service between London and Paris which was inaugurated in 1847.

The nearest competitor to the SER was the impoverished London Chatham & Dover (LC & D) and this little railway was intent upon reaching Dover, the other main cross-channel port in the south-east, for its own Continental service. The Chatham had a more difficult route to the coast through the North Downs and also had the added complication of the Government protection for the port as a strategic naval base. But for all of their flaws the railways were self-serving and actually created their own customer base. The township of Welwyn Garden City to the north of London is a latter day reminder of how the railways served the migration of people out of the crowded city to suburban houses which had gardens. In later years from around 1900 onwards, the workers in the city were able to make a daily commute by railway and for the south-east the favoured suburbs were the seaside houses on the North Kent coast.

Before this the new route to Dover had been completed in July 1861, Ramsgate would see its service commence in 1863. Had income from suburban traffic been available at this time the company may well have prospered,

but as we have seen, this only developed some years later before which the Chatham had been declared bankrupt in 1866.

The new line to the coast commenced at Holborn, went south over Blackfriars bridge to Herne Hill where it joined the original Chatham line from Victoria to Bromley and Swanley. The East Kent Railway laid lines to Strood where the Medway was bridged and the strategic naval base of Chatham was connected to the mainline. The route proceeded eastwards to Faversham (1858), Canterbury (1860) and Dover (Priory station 1861), boring through the North Downs by way of the Lydden Tunnel at Shepherdswell. The harbour station was constructed in November 1861 and the Chatham was able to commence its cross-channel services from Dover. Crucially, the company captured the lucrative Post Office mails contract in 1862 from its bitter rival, the SER. This latter company owned and maintained Folkestone as its main cross-channel port but as Dover was specified as the mail port the company had declined to renew the Post Office contract. Dover benefited greatly from its status as a military base, and as the principal of the Cinque Ports it provided pilots for the numerous sailing vessels on cross-channel voyages.

The combination of increasing traffic volumes and the bottleneck of the only rail pathway into central London from the south-east was starting to cause real problems for the resident railway companies.

There were new traffic demands being generated

Now with a four digit SR number, 1595. A Margate to Charing Cross, via Canterbury West express, photographed approaching Dumpton Park south of Broadstairs sometime in the late 1930s. *A W V Mace / Roger Carpenter*

by suburbia in the North of Kent: the tourist traffic to the Kent seaside holiday resorts, exchange passenger and goods traffic to the northern railways, goods from the ports, cement and coal from north Kent, and the cross-channel services to the Continent. This level of growth may have been good for business but the available motive power was starting to be very inadequate. The Boer War of 1899 had generated a general shortage of motive power as the goods trade surged to support the war effort. It is recorded by Mr RW Kidner that from 5pm to 6.20pm there were 33 trains booked to depart from Charing Cross for the south-east with nearly half destined for Dartford and North Kent on the Chatham line. The companies were shovelling in trains as fast as they could for these peak travelling periods. The SER built the Ewer Street depot at Metropolitan Junction, between London Bridge and Waterloo Junction, to stable empty Continental and suburban stock. The slow lines between Charing Cross and Cannon Street were filled with empty trains, running buffer to buffer, moving into the platforms as soon as they had been vacated by the departing services. In the space of eighty minutes there was a continuous run of hectic activity as trains were shuffled into the four platforms of the very small Charing Cross terminus,

to be filled to capacity and then to steam out to do battle with the spaghetti junctions of Cannon Street and London Bridge. It was noted by the Railway Magazine in 1898 that the Chairman of the SE&CR, Cosmo Bonsor, was expressing very deep regrets at not taking the opportunity to build a loop across to the northern bank of the Thames. This short line would have converted the Charing Cross and Cannon Street terminals into through stations and removed the need to reverse trains into conflicting movements at Metropolitan and Borough Junctions.

After negotiating the many crossing points and opposing trains on their way to Deptford the loaded trains then had to overcome the banks of the North Downs. The ruling gradient of about 1:300 to the coast stiffened to 1:120 from Orpington to Knockholt, and 1:160 from Dunton Green to Sevenokes * (sic) The climbs to the highest points were only made even more challenging by the long tunnels at Knockholt and Sevenokes. This really tested the locomotives as the loads increased and their small size and primitive technology did the hard-pressed engine crews no favours. The SER had the restriction of the narrow Mountfield and Wadhurst tunnels on the Hastings Line so that the locomotive and rolling stock had to be rather

The same engine, No. 1595.

narrower than permitted elsewhere. This restriction persisted into the days of British Railways until eventually the tunnels were interlaced thus giving clearance for normal stock. The Chatham mainline was noted for the severe gradients and switchbacks which demanded much sustained effort from the engine and its crew. And then, in complete contrast to the trials and tribulations of leaving the congested London stations and surmounting the North Downs, the engine crews faced a fast downhill run into the ports of Folkestone and Dover.

The operating area of the SE&CR, formed in 1899, had three main constraints, the high density of stations in London created high traffic volumes, the light trackwork and bridges on the Chatham line imposed weight restrictions whilst the small tunnels on the South Eastern Hastings line kept the dimensions of stock in check. As a consequence the 4-4-0 tender locomotive became the prevalent configuration for the SE&CR. This type offered fast running on the level and good climbing abilities in the hills They were ideal for the prestigious Continental services where good timekeeping was essential for the connections with the cross-channel ferries. As the sailor has always maintained – 'the tide is king and time waits for no man', and never more so than for a late train. The wealthy clientele paid for, and quite rightly demanded, satisfactorily results for their premium supplement fares on the Continental services. In an attempt to remedy their poor public relations the SE&CR reverted to an ornate and colourful Edwardian style for the D and E class 4-4-0 tender engines.

For the less fortunate commuter on the northern Kent lines there was little to be thankful for. In 1870 Hamilton Ellis described both companies in equal terms as 'bywords of poverty stricken inefficiency and dirtiness'. Notwithstanding the high level of traffic density there was

also the problem of short runs between the many stations in central London. The smooth running of services into and out-of the city were always critically timed and one rogue train could throw the finely balanced flow out of kilter. The ideal suburban engine was therefore light, easy to handle, reliable and quick off the mark. In the cut and thrust of the rush hour the trains had to be punctual to a fault and engine crews needed to be moving off before the station master had put his whistle away. The need for quick turnarounds in the confined spaces of the city termini meant that the suburban engine should run backwards as well as they went forwards, thus precluding the tender engine types. The engine to meet these tough challenges was the universal 0-4-4 tank and this configuration appeared in several guises and numbered many hundreds across the entire railway network.

The SER introduced their first suburban tank locomotive in 1864 with the 205 class 0-4-2T engines. The class was designed by James Cudworth and although these performed well on their duties in the city they were restricted in range due to relatively small fuel and water capacities. The twelve engines of the class were soon superseded by an enlarged version. These had larger fuel bunkers and water tanks but the resulting increase in weight meant that the single rear axle had to be replaced with a bogie to produce an 0-4-4 tank engine. The Caledonian had used this type for some years and the SER had the honour of introducing the configuration to the English commuting fraternity in 1866. The engines had compensating levers on the coupled drivers and on the bogie to equalise the weight between the axles. The 0-4-4 wheel configuration set a design trend for the archetypical suburban engine and the Cudworth designs are reputed to have produced excellent, free-steaming and robust engines, with the additional benefit

Above - Rear end detail of No. 1598.
Below - Wartime livery for No. 1599.

of smooth running from the William Adams designed bogie when pointing bunker first.

The type was to reach the zenith of performance with the H class under the supervision of Mr Harry S Wainwright. This class had an impeccable pedigree which can be traced back to the Chatham and to the A class 0-4-4T of William Kirtley in 1875. Although the equivalent design by James Stirling on the South Eastern was much newer (the Q class was built later in 1887), this latter was not considered to be a match for the former. Kirtley's A class engine was so much better that it was developed into the R class. The Chatham 0-4-4T Rs were intended to work through the Metropolitan tunnels with exchange traffic to the Great Northern. They became the darlings of the shed master for their wide route availability and were the template for a new engine for suburban and semi-fast passenger services in 1904. This became the H class of which sixty-six examples were put into service. The H has been judged as Wainwright's best engine and this accolade is borne out by the 50 years of service. The Hs were considered to be neat, attractive, robustly constructed and ideally suited to the wear and tear of the inner city tracks. The design introduced many new technical features to the SE&CR but the most noticeable cosmetic characteristic were the side extensions to the roof so that the rain strips protruded over the cab sides. This simple feature was known as the pagoda roof and it may have afforded some protection for the crew from the inevitable rain but it also became a unique design signature for the SE&C railway. The dimensions of the H pattern boiler gave a diameter of 4 foot 3 inches, and length of 10 foot 3 ½ inches. The axle loading of 16 tons 16 cwt on the driving axles gave no concerns to the South Eastern Civil Engineer for the lightly laid track of the North Kent lines. The class ranged freely over the South Eastern section on semi-fast mainline and cross-country passenger train duties. They have been spotted on the suburban trains and at the head of Continental expresses. The Chatham section had to make do with the veteran Kirtley A class 0-4-4T engines when the newer Stirling Q's were prematurely withdrawn having fallen short of the exacting performance requirements for the London suburban services.

The demise of the warring chairmen of the Chatham and South Eastern companies allowed them to operate as a single company under a unified management committee in 1899. This arrangement removed the need for duplicating and costly services, and although the companies remained as separate entities, permitted the transfer of the best people to key positions in the new SE&CR. The appointment of Wainwright to the position of Locomotive and Carriage Superintendent in 1899 greatly helped the railway to regain a sense of stability and direction. Even though Wainwright had little experience in designing locomotives the arrangement gave Mr Robert Surtees of the LC&DR to opportunity to turn out some very impressive and long-lived engines. With a proven reputation for reliability and punctual service the H design was the logical choice for further development. The boiler design was so successful that 250 examples were built and many of its predecessors, and successors, were updated with the H boiler. The boiler of dimensions 4ft 3in by 10ft 3 ½ in had a heating surface of 1,104 sq ft. The 0-6-0 'O' class goods engine, of which No 65 (on the Bluebell Railway) is an example, was so treated in 1908 to become the 'O1' class.

The need for standardisation coupled with the Civil Engineer's axle load limits (on the Chatham) and size envelope (on the Hastings line) presented a few design challenges. Wainwright proposed an upgraded 'H' class design to address the issues of limited fuel and water capacities, using the 'C' class boiler and 1,600 gallons on an 0-4-4 tank engine, to be known as the 'K' class. This boiler was slightly larger at 4ft 5 ¾ ins by 10 ft 9 ins with 1,200 sq feet of heating surface and was pressed to 160 lbs of pressure. But when the ink had dried on the design drawings it was found that the water tanks could only hold 1,300 gallons and at 60 tons, an increase of 6 tons over the H, the axle loadings of 19 tons exceeded to Engineer's weight limits for the Chatham line.

In 1906 the board of Directors noted that C class tender engines were being used in the city and thought this was inappropriate use of these powerful freight engines. With this in mind Wainwright considered converting the type into tank locos and accordingly an 0-6-2T with 1,700 gallons, and weighing in at 63 tons, was proposed. It appears that although this design came close to being approved none of the class was built. There are records of another 'C' class conversion, the S class. As a saddle tank 0-6-0 this engine must have been the closest design to what the railway needed for an effective suburban engine.

The problem of suburban motive power was now pressing as the new-fangled electric trams were offering more frequent, and indeed cleaner and quieter services in the inner city for the commuting community. The trains were being deserted by the daily travellers and to bring the matter to a conclusion Surtees produced two designs for the new suburban engine based on a six-coupled layout and the C class boiler. The new type had to contend with frequent start-stops in the city, smart timekeeping in the south London traffic flow and dense fog banks, steep climbs and descents on the flanks of the North Downs, and fast runs along the straights to Ashford and Folkestone, and to Canterbury and Dover. The proposed solutions could not have been more different with designs submitted for a large 4-6-2 tank and a smaller 0-6-4 tank engine. The designs were aimed at increasing the size of the fuel bunker and water tanks to improve range, and featured a superheater to aid performance on hills and fast sections. The large tank engine turned out to be very nose heavy, with 19 tons on the front bogie, 17, 16, and 15 tons on the coupled wheels, and 12 tons on the trailing pony truck. This design was refused for size on the Tonbridge – Hastings line and for weight by the severe limits on the Chatham. The smaller 0-6-4 tank

SECR bedfellows, the unique 'S' class 0-6-0ST and yet again No. 1595. The location is not given.

design was not immune to these restrictions and was also refused for the Chatham section but after some minor modifications was accepted to work the Hastings line. The six coupled wheel configuration without a leading bogie is quite unusual in Britain although the Irish, Metropolitan, Midland and Highland railways had small numbers in service until replacement by the more popular 2-6-4T type.

The 0-6-4T was named the 'J' class and the first five engines were delivered into service in 1913 from the Ashford Works. These were the largest tank locomotive in the SE&CR at the time. As the intended successor to the 'H' class, and looking very much like its brother from the front, the boiler was of 4 ft 5 ¾ inch diameter, 10 ft 7 ½ in long, with 160 lbs of pressure from a Belpaire firebox. The bunker was enlarged to carry 3 ½ tons of coal and 1,400 gallons of water. A further 600 gallons were carried in the two small side tanks. The pagoda roof was carried over from the H to perpetuate the sibling likeness between the classes. The class had a designed tractive effort of 20,370 lbs, giving an increase of 17 percent over the 17,360 lbs from the H class using a boiler of similar size to the C class but with a Belpaire firebox. Ashford turned out the five engines in the modified Wainwright livery of dark green with light green border. The borders were simplified from the ornate lining exhibited on the express Ds and Es. The reverse curve scallops in the corners of the bands and the fine red lines were removed, leaving a thin yellow line on the inside. The brass embellishments of the shining dome and splasher beadings had been dropped in the interests of resting the eyes of the drivers and shed crews, as well as for cost savings. The red-shaded gold letters of the SE&CR managing committee and its coat-of-arms also took their leave of the tank sides although the engine numbers in brass figures were retained on the bunker sides. This simplified livery became the new standard from October 1914.

The class were to be bolstered by five more engines and these were ordered in late 1913. However, the untimely retirement of Wainwright and the looming threat of conflict forced a reprioritisation of the locomotive building programme and the next batch of five engines was duly cancelled.

The 'Js' were intended to replace the 'Ds' and 'Es' on the semi-fast Continental trains. These two classes had been developed from the highly regarded 'M' class family of 4-4-0 locomotives from the stable of Kirtley in the LC&DR. The Continental expresses were now becoming longer and heavier trains, and at the same time the locomotives had to provide power for the electric lighting and steam heating which was being introduced into the carriages. The elegant but lightweight 4-4-0's were being overwhelmed by the demands of train and terrain.

The batch of five 'J' class engines were allocated to the Bricklayers Arms depot and assigned to duties working the Cannon Street to Tonbridge, Hastings and Dorking semi-fast trains. However, despite the impeccable pedigree of the 'H' and 'C' parentage the 'Js' were not particularly successful on these services. The combination of small driving wheels and poor steaming qualities made the class less suited for the long fast downhill runs to Hastings particularly when being worked hard. A number of modifications to the smokebox were proposed for the 'Js' and were aimed at improving steam production. Number 207 was selected as the test bed and the engine was trialled on the Charing Cross to Hastings express trains. But even with the boiler updates the 'Js' steaming capability was still inferior to the 'Hs' and the small diameter driving wheels, so crucial for smart acceleration and steady climbing abilities, were not allowing the engine to run freely for the long fast sections to the coast.

It might have been possible to revise the design of

Clearly one of the more photogenic members of the class. British Railways livery for what is now No. 31595. In early days spare engine headlamps were often carried on top of the nearside bunker nearest to the spectacle plate.

the larger 4-6-2 tank proposal to provide an alternative. But in a committee meeting in June 1913 the SE&CR had taken the reluctant step of designing a locomotive type with route availability limited for the southern section only. In tandem with this the Divisional Engineer of the Chatham was asked to make improvements to the line infrastructure and to remove the weight restrictions. Accordingly, Wainwright was instructed to enlarge the D and E class 4-4-0's (to become the SER only 'L' class), and then had been obliged to retire. The new designs were brought in by his successor, Mr Richard E L Maunsell.

The successful 'Ds', 'Es' and 'Ls' were updated (after the war) by Maunsell to give the D1 and E1 classes, and the more powerful L1 class (the latter, not appearing until 1926), but even in original form the 4-4-0s were considered better all-round performers than the 'J' tanks, and were preferred to head the fast Hastings trains from their introduction in 1914.

Consequently the 'Js' were relegated to hauling heavy suburban trains out of London to Redhill and Tonbridge. In the early years of the Great War the 'Js' were generally used for workmen's trains to Croydon. The trains carried production workers to the munitions and armaments factories and their numbers were greatly increased as the production of war materials ramped up to full output. Numbers 597 and 614 were transferred to Redhill in October of 1915 for the Cannon Street trains, and were also used on the Reading branch hauling goods trains to the Great Western (GWR) railway. From the beginning of this transfer service in 1898 the SER had real difficulties on the steeply graded Redhill to Reading section. The Stirling 'O' class 0-6-0 goods engine proved to be underpowered for a standard 30-wagon load and frequently had to stop to raise steam. The most numerous freight vans were filled with

products of Huntley and Palmers and it would not be palatable for slow biscuits to delay the busy passenger services. Shortly afterwards the two 'J' class engines made the reverse trip back to Tonbridge to work the Hastings line whilst number 129 was used to trial the bogie of the new K class 2-6-4T between October 1916 and November 1917.

From August 1915 the 'Js' were in the standard austerity livery of plain light green with yellow lettering and without the shiny brass bits. The cost of painting was reduced further by leaving the paintwork unvarnished but after a short time the green paint and yellow lettering had become indistinguishable. The signalmen were unable to identify services by the train number and the remedy was to use unlined light grey and white lettering. In 1916 the 'J' class tanks were thus repainted and in service this livery weathered down to dark grey.

The end of the war in 1918 saw two of the 'Js' return to the Hastings line to head the fast business expresses once again. The absence of any form of maintenance or replacement during the war had worn out the venerable 4-4-0 tender engines. But even though the two 'Js', numbers 597 and 614, generally kept good time on these demanding services the crews preferred the more capable and powerful 'L' class. 'J' class engines 207, 597 and 611 were transferred to Reading for working the GWR transfer duties and remained on these services until the autumn of 1926 when the K or 'River' class 2-6-4T types replaced them.

At the grouping in 1923 the band of five 'Js' passed into the ownership of the Southern and received the new plain green livery. From February 1929 the class were usefully employed on the London Bridge to Tunbridge Wells and Tonbridge via Redhill services. These trains were very well patronised so the 'Js' were at last fulfilling their design brief to haul heavy trains. With the construction of the Hither Green depot in December 1933 the whole class was transferred in and worked the empty stock trains into Charing Cross and Cannon Street. The electrification of the Sevenoaks line in 1935 made the class redundant again, and they were moved to Ashford to partner their smaller brothers, the 'H' class.

The 'Js' were also occasionally used on Brighton excursions in place of the usual 'D' or 'L' class engines and, twenty-two years on, proved that the original design concept was sound. From 1936 the class were used on goods trains to Tonbridge – Hastings route until replaced by 'N1' moguls. For reasons unknown the 1937 Engine Restriction Book put the brake on the 'Js' when the class was prohibited from the Ashford – Hastings line. It was only another conflict which kept the engines out of the scrapyard and extinction.

In 1939 the dark green livery gave way to unlined black with green lined golden numerals on the bunkers. At this time the covers for the piston valve tailrods, which had protruded though the front buffer beams, were removed on four of the five engines. Engine 207 retained the covers and rods, although over the next few years the snifting valves were removed from behind the chimneys on all of the engines. The Second World War saw all five 'Js' back at Ashford on the Maidstone to Margate services. During the evacuation of the army from Dunkirk in the June of 1940, the 'Js' were recalled to pilot the heavy troop trains to Orpington. Engines 207 (SR1595) and 597 (SR1597) were loaned to Tonbridge to provide the heavy lift capability needed for these war saving services.

With the end of the war and in BR ownership the five locos were renumbered 31595 to 31599, and of these numbers 31595 (SECR 207) and 31596 (SECR 129) were painted in BR lined black. Just one year later the engines of the 'J' class were being replaced by LMS class 4 Fairburn 2-6-4Ts. The 'Js' were scrapped as they were replaced and number 1596 (SECR129) was steamed last in September 1951.

The small band of locomotives were intended to have an impossibly wide operational capability, and had to work on the congested city lines and in the open countryside. The engine design was compromised by size limits on the Hastings line and by weight limits over the Medway on the Chatham. The tiny space of the southern London inner termini prevented engine turning, and by precluding tenders therefore limited fuel and water, and their range. As a consequence the type was being worked at the very limit of its capabilities. It cannot be surprising that the crews preferred the larger and more powerful tender locomotives for the ease of surmounting the 'South Eastern's mountain branch', as Mr Bradley has termed the SER mainline. But nevertheless, in times of conflict and stress, the 'Js' were capable of, and used for, hauling all sorts of trains. And did so in the area for which they were designed, on the lines to Hastings and Folkestone. The 'J'

class, the little known engine class, was an unusual type with an impressive history for appearing all over the South Eastern network. The class was in service for 38 years as the forgotten maid of all trades.

* The original spelling from the family name of Sir William Sevenokes who founded the town in the 15th Century, and which was chartered by Queen Elizabeth.

Locomotive History:

Built	SECR	SR 1927/8	BR	Withdrawn
Oct 1913	129	A596 - 1596	31596	Sep 1951
Oct 1913	207	A595 - 1595	31595	Apr 1951
Nov 1913	597	A597 - 1597	31597	Oct 1950
Nov 1913	611	A598 - 1598	31598	Jan 1951
Dec 1913	614	A599 - 1599	31599	Oct 1949

Sources:

DL Bradley: Railway Magazine, August 1958.
DL Bradley: Locomotive History of the South Eastern Railway.
DL Bradley, Locomotives of the London, Chatham and Dover Railway, 1960
JH Russell: Pictorial Record of Southern Railway locomotives, 1991.
WAT Aves: Locomotives Illustrated: 169 – locos built SR works Ashford part 2.
Various Authors: Southern Railway E-Group.
Various Authors: Wikipedia.
RW Kidner, The South Eastern & Chatham Railway, Oakwood, 1963.
Neil Sprinks, Out and About on the Chatham, Steam days, June 2009.
Stanley Jenkins, Steam Days at Dover, Steam Days, November 2008.
David Glasspool, KentRail.org.com
Railway Magazine, 1898, Illustrated interview No 11 - Mr Henry Cosmo Orme Bonsor MP.
George Measom, Illustrated Guide to the South Eastern Railway, 1853.
David Harvey, The Remembrance Line Association, theremembranceline.org.uk
South Eastern & Chatham Railway Society, Centenary Album, 1999.
Adrian Gray, The South Eastern & Chatham Railway, 1998.
John K Walton: British Seaside: Holidays and Resorts in the 20th Century, 2005.

Again in his own words, "Brighton Station 60 years ago. Billington 'E5' 0-6-2T 'Wanborough' awaits the signal to move from Platform 6. On the East side a Stroudley 'D1' 0-4-2T waits with a Tunbridge Wells line service. (Note unusual feature of distant signals at the entrance to a terminus. When 'off' these indicated the platform road was clear right down to the buffer stops.)

IN RETROSPECT AT BRIGHTON

H M Madgwick

Standing on Brighton's No. 1 West Side platform recently surveying the barren and derelict waste of open ground, all that remains of the once busy running sheds following the demolitions carried out as a result of the demise of steam, one can but reflect upon the contrasting present scene to that of the station in the first decade of the Century.

Brighton was perhaps, the finest of all terminal stations outside London. Whilst originally little more than a huddle of low-roofed wooden train sheds, the L.B.&.S.C.Rly's. major rebuilding scheme for Brighton of 1882 produced an imposing and well laid out station.

This was no easy task, for the original site had been cut into the side of a steep chalk hill presenting limited space for extension. However, the difficult operation was performed and from that date onwards, the great girdered twin roof spans have towered over and dominated the surrounding streets. This vast glazed roofing shelters the eleven platforms from which, almost around the clock, came the west Main, East and West Coast Branch line trains with a variety of locomotives that must have been a delight to the train catchers of that bygone age.

One of the present writer's earliest recollections is of visits to an Aunt whose house overlooked the running sheds and station from a wonderful viewpoint on Terminus Hill. One was scarcely inside the house before permission was being sought to leave the elders and repair to the first floor bedroom window, there to remain, one hoped, for the duration of the visit, fascinated by the bustle of railway activity being unfolded in a wide panorama below .

What a scene of contrast this was to the present day operations. Whereas now, even the 'Brighton Belle', as with all electric trains, creeps in and out with possibly a flatulent hoot, the departure of its counterpart of half a century ago was attended by the greatest activity. The arrival firstly of the station pilot with the rake of cars, then the main line engine coming off the shed where, for some time beforehand one could watch it being scrupulously prepared, finally to back down cautiously on the train. The signals clearing as the outgoing road was set up and then the great moment of departure with all the impressive effect of steam power as an accompaniment.

Over on the East Side the Locomotive Works was then a bustling hive of activity wherein the plans of Stroudley, Billinton and Marsh had all taken form and emerged with the elegance of design and perfection of workmanship associated with the great days of railways. From here the artisans poured out in their hundreds to their homes in the streets surrounding the works at the behest of the lunch time hooter.

Now the great long shops stand dark and deserted, stripped clean, their only sound being the mournful sighing of the wind through this sad and cold place.

The five signal boxes controlling the approaches and movements in and out of the station through Saxby and Farmer's equipment were a source of fascination in themselves.

To stand in the evening dusk and glimpse the signalmen, outlined in the yellow gaslight, operating the variously coloured levers to the ringing of the gongs and bells, with the red and green semaphore lights changing in response to their moves is surely indeed a part of that mysterious essence compounded in the fascination of the railway scene of the past, lost to-day in the cold and clinical atmosphere of electronics in signalling.

Outside the station, even as to-day, although masked by the steelwork of the forecourt awning, stood David Mocatta's splendid original Italianate façade. This from its upper story, commanded a view seaward down the Queen's Road hill, up which all day long trotted the horse

---

The name H M Madgwick will need no introduction to any student of the Brighton - or indeed the Southern.

Photographs of his taking and his collection have graced many a book in the past, although probably until now, little has been known of the man himself.

Recently unearthed in a dusty archive was a short typed eulogy relative to his own memories of Brighton station itself. It is reproduced here in its entirety, together with opposite, the one image that accompanied the pages.

H M Madgwick's description of times past are of an era we can only know of through photographs, whilst his blunt comments of the present - itself half a century ago present an interesting comparison.

We present his words in their entirety. I suspect by the time you have reached the bottom of the next page you will agree that successive generations have lost more than most would have appreciated.

'growlers' to enter the station through the cavernous cab tunnel which still remains as a gloomy subterranean cobbled passage.

Whilst the smell of gas lamps, wet straw and horses has departed from this eerie place, one feels that the ghosts of those old cabbies might well haunt it, wrapped around in their many top coats and horse blankets and, each one wearing the official L.B.&.S.C Rly. numbered brass oval badge. The insignia of their authority to ply for hire within the station limits.

Close by the tunnel exit stood the station fire engine in its glass panelled shed, brass-work gleaming and bearing the bold L.B.S.C.R monogram. This fine old horse -drawn appliance was built by Shand Mason in 1877. Unfortunately sold and, it is believed, dismantled by the purchasers in 1929, probably for the value of its brasswork, it would have been a fine vintage piece to-day had but someone been far sighted enough to preserve it.

The high spot of the morning traffic was the stately departure of the up 'City Limited'. This was in marked contrast to the hectic business traffic rush witnessed to-day for its passengers were not largely composed of the typists, clerks and minor management people who scurry to and from London daily under the appellation of 'Commuters'. Season Ticket holders and very First Class at that were the people expressly catered for by the 'Limited' long before the term was Americanised. Top hats, frock coats and a dignified progress by single and pair horse carriages to and from the station was the order of the day for was not this train the important link between the mansions in Brighton's Regency Squares and the seats of power in the City of London?

Over in the Running Sheds was a sight to behold indeed. Brighton, being the major locomotive depot outside London, housed an extensive stud which, with visiting engines, always presented a wide variety of classes.

On a Summer Sunday morning, with incoming excursion traffic at its peak, thirty to forty engines could be seen out in the yard alone, not counting those Inside the sheds. What names, ringing with the pride of Imperial England, they bore, 'Emperor', 'Empress', 'Sirdar', 'Canada', 'Australia', together with Statesmen, Soldiers and the great Engineers. There too were engines carrying the names of the Southern English Counties and those of the quiet villages and hamlets of the lovely Sussex countryside which was so much the 'Brighton' Railway's own preserve.

There was just one illustration accompanying Madgwick's piece - that seen on page 94`. But this was an opportunity too good to miss and it is with pleasure that we reproduce a few more from his collection showing the cab road and with it an indication of the slope upon which the terminus was built. Madwick's own comments of, "gas lamps, wet straw and horses" are well described.   *With grateful thanks to Antony Ford for illustrations.*

Brighton interior.

What individual things the L.B.S.C locomotives were, each and almost every one, excepting the purely Goods Engines, with its name lifting it above the slight identity secured by a mere number.

One final, but lasting memory. Outside the station on the forecourt there stood, until the '20s at least a real old fashioned Coffee Stall.

To stand and partake of a steaming pint mug of cocoa with a hunk of crisp fresh bread and cheese or a sizzling sausage, the cold of a winter's night banished by the warmth and glow of the cosy interior, and surrounded by its cheery patrons with their good humoured banter was surely something no modern clattering cafeteria with its neon lights and plastic wrapped rubber crusted substitute for sandwiches can offer.

Now all is gone. Where once the high vaulted glass roof echoed the Stroudley whistles only the electrics hoot and the diesels chatter, replacing the characteristic indefinable smell of the steam locomotive with their nauseous oily stench.

Doubtless the day will come when all that will remain of the erstwhile L.B.S.C system will be its trunk and possibly its Eastern and Western coastal extremities. It may well be that the station itself will be moved to a new site. However this may be, for those who knew the Brighton Railway in its heyday, remains the consolation that all the changes this present age is bringing cannot efface the memories of what was indeed, in its prime, one of the great stations of this Country.

We know it happened, we know how and when it occurred - the working time table often gives details of which services will supply stores (coal and water) to outlying signal boxes. From the same source we even know which (supervising) station was responsible for providing those supplies. But how many times was it recorded on film? Probably very few.

Here a Brockenhurst porter has been given the job of delivering supplies to Lymington Junction. No doubt considered a nice easy number, "Ride on the train and drop off a couple of bags on the way out. Apart from a few minutes of work you can put your feet up for half-an-hour…" Really!

THE SOUTHERN WAY Issue No 20

On 12 July 1949, a Portland to Weymouth train leaves Rodwell in charge of 'O2' No. 30177 complete with (GWR coaching stock.

100

COLOUR INTERLUDE

Memories of the Southern west of Exeter. On 15 May 1975 the Battle of Britain Locomotive Society organised the 'Atlantic Coast Express' tour hauled regretfully not by a B of B pacific but instead by a pair of Class 25 diesels - for the record Nos. 25244 and 25161. The train is seen here at Barnstaple Junction, already showing the ravages of rationalisation but nothing to how it would appear years later - that subject is best left alone. One of the participants on the tour was Martin Body, some of whose 'Withered Arm' and 'S & D' images feature on this and the subsequent two pages. Martin comments, "...incidentally, that was the trip that allowed my father and myself to remove one of the three running-in boards which we had previously bought, and by prior arrangement put it in the guard's van, no doubt to the surprise of many of the tour participants." "Please Sir, can anyone have a nameboard...?"

Above - *Sunshine at least at Templecombe Lower Platform - S & D. The loco shed is the middle distance. How just over a decade makes a difference. This was 1974, yet ten years before, trains would pass between Bath and Bournemouth..... .*

Left - *Ashwater between Halwill to Launceston. Taken in early 1984 it was already 18 years since trains had called - yet there still a milk churn!*

No prizes for identifying Barnstaple Town, or rather the remnants thereof - station and also looking east towards the bridge. Services had ceased in October 1970 and this was the scene four years later shortly before track lifting commenced.

All views - Martin Body.

Further images of this type will be found in our books:

'In the Tracks of the Ace'. the 'Impermanent Ways' series, and also the various 'Sabotaged and Defeated' volumes.

'Winter Memories' by George Hobbs. SECR P class 0-6-0T No. 753 (SR No. 556, later No. A556, later No. 1566, BR No. 31556) as 'Pride of Sussex at Robertsbridge, 27 December 1970. Withdrawn in April 1961, it was to have a further lease of life being sold in June 1961 to James Hodson & Sons, Millers, of Robertsbridge where it was named as seen and continued to perform on the mill sidings as well as collecting and delivering vehicles to the BR yard at Robertsbridge station . With a change of ownership at the mill, rail connection ceased and the locomotive passed to the Kent & East Sussex Railway in 1970. It has since undergone two complete overhauls in preservation and currently reposes in the livery of the SECR, its first owners.